Whatever It Takes: How Professional Learning Communities Respond When Kids Don't Learn

Richard DuFour
Rebecca DuFour
Robert Eaker
Gayle Karhanek

Solution Tree

Copyright © 2004 by Solution Tree
(formerly National Educational Service)
304 West Kirkwood Avenue
Bloomington, Indiana 47404
(812) 336-7700
(800) 733-6786 (toll free)
FAX: (812) 336-7790
e-mail: info@solution-tree.com
www.solution-tree.com

Cover design by Grannan Graphic Design, Ltd.
Text design by T.G. Design Group

Printed in the United States of America

ISBN 978-1-932127-28-7

Dedication

We dedicate this book to our parents:

William DuFour and Colleen Van Ness
Russell and Pearl Burnette
Raymond and Jewell Eaker

Like all parents, they sent their sons and daughters to school with the hope that their children would enter an environment that was both compassionate and challenging, a culture in which students were valued as individuals and stretched to achieve their full potential. It is our hope that this book will assist educators in their efforts to create such a culture in their own schools, and in doing so, help realize the hopes and dreams of parents of every generation.

—Richard DuFour, Rebecca DuFour, and Robert Eaker

To Janet for her assistance in preparation of the manuscript, to Sam for his love and support for over two decades, and to my family who taught me that we can change the world one individual at a time.

—Gayle Karhanek

Table of Contents

About the Authors

Richard DuFour, Ed.D, is recognized as a leader in helping school practitioners apply the principles of Professional Learning Communities in their schools. During his tenure as superintendent of Adlai Stevenson High School District 125 in Lincolnshire, Illinois, Stevenson became one of the most recognized and celebrated high schools in America. Rick received his state's highest award as both a principal and superintendent and was presented both the Distinguished Alumni Award of Illinois State University and the Distinguished Scholar Practitioner Award of the University of Illinois. He has authored 5 books and more than 50 professional articles. He developed the video series on the principalship for the Association of Supervision and Curriculum Development and is a featured columnist for the *Journal of Staff Development.* Rick is an international consultant who has worked with professional organizations, school districts, universities, and state departments of education.

Rebecca DuFour, M.Ed., is a former elementary school principal who helped her school earn state and national recognition as a model Professional Learning

Community. Becky is one of the featured principals in *Video Journal of Education's* program "Leadership in the Age of Standards and High Stakes" (2001). She is also the lead consultant and featured principal for *Video Journal of Education's* "Elementary Principals as Leaders of Learning" (2003). Becky is co-author of *Getting Started: Reculturing Schools to Become Professional Learning Communities* (2002), has written for numerous professional journals, and serves as a book reviewer for the *Journal of Staff Development*. She is an international consultant who has worked for professional organizations, school districts, universities, and state departments of education.

Robert Eaker, Ed.D., is the former executive vice-president and provost at Middle Tennessee State University. Bob has written widely on the issues of effective teaching, effective schools, helping teachers use research findings, and high expectations and student achievement. He is co-author of *Creating the New American School* (1992), *Professional Learning Communities at Work* (1998), and *Getting Started: Reculturing Schools to Become Professional Learning Communities* (2002). He has spoken at numerous national meetings, such as the National Association of Secondary School Principals and the Association for Supervision and Curriculum Development, and he was chosen by Phi Delta Kappa for the "People in Educational Evaluation and Research" interview series that appeared in the October 1986 issue of *Phi Delta Kappan*. Bob regularly consults with school districts throughout the nation on school improvement issues.

Gayle A. Karhanek, M.Ed., has served as the director of student services at Adlai Stevenson High School in Lincolnshire, Illinois, since 1979. Adlai Stevenson has been selected as one of America's best high schools on twelve separate occasions and has won four coveted Blue Ribbon Awards of Excellence from the United States Department of Education. She won the "Those Who Excel" Award from the Illinois State Board of Education in 2000 and has worked with districts throughout the United States to create cost-effective interventions to meet the academic, behavioral, and social-emotional needs of students. As author of Stevenson's Pyramid of Interventions, she understands that a systematic approach is the only way to meet the specific, individualized needs of all students in your school, at the same time, and in the same way.

Foreword

The Power of Collective Intelligence

W*hatever It Takes: How Professional Learning Communities Respond When Kids Don't Learn* is a landmark book—and a timely one. Taken together, the stories that fill its pages are a testament to what schools most need now: to begin systematically harnessing the power of collective intelligence that already resides in the school to solve problems.

We still underestimate this need. Fortunately, the stories in this book compel us to see that the combination of commitment and collective intelligence can redefine what is possible in our schools. All we need to do is work hard to honor and organize the creative capacities of school-based teacher teams, of authentic "learning communities."

Henry Ford once said that his success was merely a function of solving one simple, manageable problem at a time—and that anyone could do this. The challenge is to stay with it, and to do so in pursuit of a vision no less grand than anything Ford ever accomplished: to actually live up to our mission and vision statements that glibly proclaim that "all children will learn."

But will they, really? This will only be accomplished, as the authors demonstrate, by systematically and *aggressively* identifying and solving problems as they emerge; by creating "places of action, experimentation, and a willingness to test ideas that seem to hold potential for improving student achievement." As you will see, "experimentation" for them is no flimsy notion; it must be characterized by ongoing observation, monitoring, measurement, and adjustments until real progress and real results can be seen.

The stories of how the featured schools encountered and solved these problems make for great reading. Consider a sample of the objections and problems these schools overcame. You may recognize some of them:

- There is not enough money or personnel to provide systematic tutoring for kids who need it.

- Kids will not attend summer school or after-school tutoring; they're apathetic—or afraid of being "stigmatized."

- There is not enough time for frequent teacher collaboration.

- It is impossible—or too time-consuming—to provide grades every 6 weeks or progress reports every 3 weeks.

- We cannot honor or identify good teaching. That will only lead to unhealthy competition and bad feelings among teachers.

- The teacher's association and their contract will not allow it.

You will read about how these schools met such challenges and many more—fairly, effectively, and sometimes with breathtaking simplicity and common sense. These challenges were not met all at once or by forcing conformity, but by involving all members of the learning community—including and especially the teacher's association.

They worked on such problems thoughtfully, collectively, and continuously. Sometimes they abandoned seemingly promising but ineffective strategies; sometimes they adjusted them—and experienced great results (my favorite stories). In such an atmosphere, they sometimes abandoned an *effective* solution because a better one emerged deep into their implementation. Fortune favors the experimental mind.

This is the stuff of excellent, ever-improving organizations. But note as well that these schools made astonishing progress *with existing amounts of time and funding*. They did not wait for someone from the outside to give them the magic formula, the perfect program, or more resources. These schools found a way. They worked with what they had while inventing, innovating, and adjusting their way toward excellence. As you will see, each has made monumental—and surprisingly rapid—strides toward achieving the elusive goal of "learning for all."

Michael Fullan has written about the culture of "dependency" among school personnel—that we tend to wait for solutions from outside. These authors tell us that instead of looking "out the window," we need to look "in the mirror" at what *we* can do right now, always with the expectation of making discernible progress in the short *and* the long term. Although having money is terrific, the brutal fact is that it is no substitute for the actions and efforts most apt to improve teaching and learning. These are matters of structure and practice, of the need to replace tired, widely discredited "improvement planning" models with something far more potent, straightforward, and rare: true learning communities. The key is to give the highest priority to structures that allow educators to work as members of true research teams and thus to become, as Fullan notes, "scientists who continuously develop their intellectual and investigative capacities" (Sparks, 2003, p. 55).

Whatever It Takes is brimming with practical wisdom and inspiring stories of what happens when schools take this "intellectual and investigative" role seriously in the pursuit of "learning for all." This book will help us shed the self-imposed limitations that now hold us back. *Whatever It Takes* will make a mighty and enduring contribution to helping us create the best schools we have ever had.

—Mike Schmoker
Author, Speaker, and Consultant
Flagstaff, AZ

Introduction

An Unprecedented Challenge

"Change in schools is much more urgently needed than most teachers and school administrators seem to realize. Indeed, I believe that if schools are not changed in dramatic ways very soon, public schools will not be a vital component of America's system of education in the 21st Century."

—Phil Schlechty, 1997, p. xi

"Quality teaching requires strong professional learning communities. Collegial interchange, not isolation, must become the norm for teachers. Communities of learning can no longer be considered utopian; they must become the building blocks that establish a new foundation for America's schools."

—National Commission on Teaching, 2003, p. 17

Public school educators in the United States are now required to do something they have never before been asked to accomplish: ensure high levels of learning for all students. This mandate is not only unprecedented; it is at odds with the original goal of schools. The notion of all students learning at high levels would have been inconceivable to the pioneers of public education. If contemporary educators are to make significant progress in meeting this new challenge, they must first recognize that the institutions in which they work were not designed to accomplish the task of learning for all. They must then acknowledge the need to make fundamental changes in both the practices of their schools and the assumptions that drive those practices.

Professional Learning Communities: A Quick Review

Our earlier works present the premise that the Professional Learning Community (PLC) offers the most powerful conceptual model for transforming schools to meet their new challenges. We suggested that PLCs differ from more traditional schools in the following substantive ways:

Shared Mission, Vision, Values, and Goals

Educators in PLCs embrace the notion that the fundamental purpose of school is learning, not teaching—an enormous distinction. This emphasis on learning leads those within the school to concentrate their effort and energy on three critical questions:

1. What is it we want all students to learn—by grade level, by course, and by unit of instruction?

2. How will we know when each student has acquired the intended knowledge and skills?

3. How will we respond when students experience initial difficulty so that we can improve upon current levels of learning?

Educators in PLCs examine the practices and procedures of their schools to ensure alignment with this fundamental purpose of learning for all students, and they maintain an unrelenting focus on student learning. They develop a shared sense of the school they hope to become to better fulfill the purpose of learning for all. They articulate the collective commitments they are prepared to make to move the school toward their shared vision. They establish specific, measurable goals to serve as targets and timelines on their journey. This shared understanding of mission, vision, values, and goals represents the very foundation of a PLC and is embedded in the hearts and minds of people throughout the school.

Collaborative Teams

The basic structure of the PLC is composed of collaborative teams whose members work *interdependently* to achieve *common goals*. The team is the engine that drives the PLC effort. Some organizations base their improvement strategies on efforts to enhance the knowledge and skills of individuals. Although individual growth is essential for organizational growth to take place, it does not guarantee organizational growth. Building a school's capacity to learn is a collective rather than an individual task. People who engage in collaborative team learning are able to learn from one another and thus create momentum to fuel continued improvement. It is difficult to overstate the importance of collaborative teams in the improvement process.

Collective Inquiry

The teams of a PLC are organized to engage in collective inquiry into both best practice and the current reality regarding their students' existing levels of achievement. The people in such a school are relentless in examining and questioning the status quo, seeking new methods, testing those methods, and then reflecting on the results. Not only do they have an acute sense of curiosity and openness to new possibilities; they also recognize that the process of searching for answers is more important than having an answer.

Action Orientation and Experimentation

PLCs are action oriented. Members of such organizations turn aspirations into action and visions into reality. Not only do they act, but they are unwilling to tolerate inaction. They recognize that learning always occurs in a context of taking action, and they value engagement and experience as the most effective strategies for deep learning. In fact, the very reason that teachers work together in teams and engage in collective inquiry is to serve as a catalyst for action. The educators in a PLC recognize that until they "do differently," there is little reason to expect improved results. Furthermore, by acting in new ways, members of a PLC acquire new experiences that lead to new awareness. Gradually, this heightened awareness is assimilated into fundamental shifts in attitudes and beliefs, which, over time, transform the culture of the school.

Continuous Improvement

A persistent disquiet with the status quo and a constant search for a better way represent the heart of a PLC. Systematic processes engage each member of the organization in the consideration of several key questions:

1. What is our fundamental purpose?

2. What do we hope to become?

3. What are our strategies for getting better?

4. By what criteria will we assess our improvement efforts?

The goal is not simply learning a new system, but creating conditions for perpetual learning. It is an environment in which innovation and experimentation are not viewed as tasks to be accomplished or projects to be completed; rather they become ways of conducting day-to-day business—*forever*. In short, becoming a learning community is less like getting in shape than staying in shape; it is not a fad diet but a commitment to an essential, healthier way of life.

Results Orientation

Finally, a PLC realizes that all of its efforts in these other areas—shared mission, vision, values, and goals; collaborative teams; collective inquiry; action orientation; and continuous improvement—must be assessed on the basis of results rather than intentions. Unless initiatives are subjected to ongoing assessment on the basis of tangible results, they represent random groping in the dark rather than purposeful improvement. As Peter Senge concludes, "The rationale for any strategy for building a learning organization revolves around the premise that such organizations will produce dramatically improved results" (1995, p. 44).

Leaders of PLCs promote this focus on results by using technology to provide all staff with timely, relevant, user-friendly information that enables individuals, teams, and the school at large to identify strengths and weaknesses in areas of student learning. That information drives the action research and continuous improvement processes for individual teachers and collaborative teams.

This brief description summarizes the parameters of PLCs, but it does not convey an important final point: The PLC model is designed to touch the heart. Psychologists tell us that we share certain fundamental needs—the need to feel successful in our work, the need to feel a sense of belonging, and the need to live a life of significance by making a difference. The PLC speaks to each of these needs.

Narrowing the Focus to a Critical Question

In *Professional Learning Communities at Work: Best Practices for Enhancing Student Achievement* (DuFour & Eaker, 1998), we present the research base that supports the PLC concept and use a broad brush to paint a picture of PLCs. In *Getting Started: Reculturing Schools to Become Professional Learning Communities* (Eaker, DuFour, & DuFour, 2002), we elaborate on the concept and attempt to answer many of the questions that arise when a school begins the journey toward becoming a PLC. In this book, we narrow the focus still further to concentrate upon one of the most challenging aspects of becoming a PLC. Even if a staff has accepted learning as the fundamental purpose of their school, even if teachers are working together collaboratively to clarify exactly what each student must learn, even if they develop a variety of common assessments to monitor each student's learning, eventually that staff will face an inescapable question: *What happens in our school when, despite our best efforts in the classroom, a student does not learn?*

We contend that in traditional schools the response to that question has been left to the discretion of individual classroom teachers who are free to respond in very different ways. The support a student will (or will not) receive will depend on the practices of his or her teacher. The premise of this book is that a PLC will not leave this critical question to each teacher to resolve. A PLC will, instead, create a school-wide system of interventions that provides all students with additional time and support when they experience initial difficulty in their learning.

When considering its response to students who are experiencing difficulty, a school that purports to be a PLC should be able to answer the following questions in the affirmative:

- Is our response based upon **INTERVENTION** rather than remediation? Does the plan provide students with additional time and support for learning as soon as they experience difficulty rather than rely on remediation— summer school, retention, remedial courses—when students fail to meet a standard at the conclusion of a course or grade level?

- Is our response **SYSTEMATIC**? Have we created processes that ensure we respond to students according to a school-wide plan rather than according to the discretion of individual teachers? Are procedures in place to monitor the execution of the plan? Are all staff members aware of the procedures? Do we provide consistent responses if asked to explain the steps our school takes when students have difficulty in learning?

- Is our response **TIMELY**? How quickly are we as a school able to identify students who need additional time and support? How often do we ask the question,

"How do we know if our students are not learning?" and how quickly are we able to respond when a student has been identified?

- Is our response **DIRECTIVE**? Do we *invite* students to seek additional help or does our systematic plan *require* students to receive the additional assistance and devote the extra time necessary to master the concept? A decade of research into the "things that matter most" in raising student achievement found that the schools that improved the most insisted students get extra help whenever there was evidence that those students were having difficulty in learning (Bottoms, 1998).

Examining Our Stories

It has been said that man is a story-seeking animal. The world's cultures and religions have been handed down through the ages in the form of stories—parables, legends, fables, and allegories. Furthermore, each of us has developed our own personal story that we tell ourselves every day. As Noel Tichy (1997) writes:

> We all have world views—a complex web of ideas, values, and assumptions about how the world operates. We all have certain fundamental beliefs, for example, about whether people are naturally generous or greedy, or whether we are the victims of our fate or controllers of our own destinies. (p. 59)

One of the challenges of becoming a PLC is examining and changing the stories we tell ourselves in schools. Peter Senge (1994) contends that building a learning organization requires "a never-ever ending process whereby people in the organization articulate common stories around purpose, values, and why their work matters" (p. 298). Therefore, we have attempted to provide illustrations of important distinctions between traditional schools and PLCs through the vehicle of stories, which we hope will resonate with school practitioners.

Chapter 1 will examine the current mandate that all students learn at high levels and will place that mandate in a historical context by examining the assumptions that have guided public education. The chapter extends the popular rallying cry that "all children can learn" by re-examining the three critical questions with which all PLCs grapple in order to give that phrase relevance.

Chapter 2 describes how schools have traditionally responded when students do not learn and provides a case study to examine that response. The chapter also presents some caveats readers must keep in mind as they consider creating a system of interventions for students in their own schools.

Chapter 3 describes in detail the system of interventions created by Adlai Stevenson High School in suburban Chicago, one of three schools in the nation to receive the United States Department of Education's Blue Ribbon Award on four occasions. This system, the Pyramid of Interventions, represents a conscious attempt by the Stevenson staff to give students additional time and support when they experience difficulty in their learning.

Chapter 4 discusses some of the logistical barriers Stevenson faced in building the Pyramid and strategies for overcoming those barriers. It acknowledges that other schools in other settings will face their own unique barriers but contends that if staff members clarify their priority and focus on the right questions, they too can overcome the obstacles posed by their local context.

Chapter 5 examines the unique aspects of the middle school and explains how one of America's most celebrated middle schools has raised student performance by focusing on student achievement, building a collaborative culture, and creating systems to provide students with additional time and support.

Chapters 6 and 7 describe how a system of interventions works for students in two very different elementary schools—one in a rural setting in south-central Virginia and another in an ethnically diverse Title One school in southern California.

Chapter 8 identifies the commonalities between the four very different schools explored in the earlier chapters. It discusses how all of the characteristics of a PLC came to thrive in each school and describes some of the common approaches to leadership that characterized the principals of these four schools.

Chapter 9 examines some of the philosophical concerns that have been raised regarding the proposal to provide students with additional time and support for learning when students fail to make the effort necessary to be successful. The chapter then attempts to address each of these concerns.

Chapter 10 identifies some of the cultural shifts a school must make on the journey to becoming a Professional Learning Community. It contends that a PLC creates a "stretch culture" that leads both students and staff to embrace high expectations and to develop a sense of self-efficacy. It suggests strategies to promote such a culture.

The appendix provides artifacts from the four schools described in this book that practitioners may find helpful— mission and vision statements, job descriptions, sample correspondence, program descriptions, and graphics to illustrate intervention plans.

Whatever It Takes: Restoring Hope

The first rule of the Hippocratic Oath that has guided the medical profession for over two thousand years is "Do no harm." Rick Stiggins (2003) contends that the first rule of the educational profession should be, "Do not deprive of hope." Unfortunately, the way in which the current legislation is being applied in many schools is depriving students of hope. Students who have struggled in the past recognize that the bar is being raised higher and higher and ultimately conclude that school does not offer them a place for success and affirmation. Just as tragically, their teachers are also losing hope of meeting the tougher standards being imposed upon their schools.

The ideas presented in this book represent an attempt to restore hope. Our goal is not to offer advice as to how a school can raise test scores a few points in order to avoid sanctions. Our goal is to remind educators of the dreams and aspirations of the children who come to school, the parents who send them there, and the teachers and principals who entered the profession to make a difference in the lives of students. None of these constituencies strives for failure. Each yearns for success. Hope has a human face. The most powerful fuel for sustaining the initiative to improve a school is not the desire to raise test scores but rather the moral imperative that comes with the desire to fulfill the hopes of those we serve and those with whom we work. We remain convinced that the Professional

Learning Community concept offers the best strategy for connecting educators to that moral imperative, and we hope that this book offers helpful insights for teachers and principals who are committed to bringing the PLC concept to life in their own schools.

Chapter 1

From "Learning for the Few" to "All Kids Can Learn" to "All Kids Will Learn—Or Else!"

"Life can only be understood backwards; but it must be lived forwards."

—Søren Kierkegaard

"We can, whenever we choose, successfully teach all children whose schooling is of interest to us. We already know more than we need to do that. Whether or not we do it must finally depend on how we feel about the fact that we haven't so far."

—Ron Edmonds, 1982

As the latest wave of educational reform washes upon the public schools of the United States in the form of the No Child Left Behind (NCLB) legislation, veteran educators are finding it difficult to avoid becoming cynical. The notion that the nation's system is broken and needs to be fixed is not new. Almost 50 years ago the Russian launching of Sputnik led reformers such as Hyman Rickover to claim the failure of the public schools had not only caused the United States to fall behind Russia in the space race, but also threatened our demise in the Cold War. When the United States went on to land men on the moon, establish clear supremacy in space, and win the Cold War, schools received none of the credit.

Twenty years ago the Nation at Risk initiative (1983) asserted it was the failure of public schools that had caused the United States economy to lose ground to other nations. The report made repeated references to "decline," "deficiencies," "plight," "threats," and "risks" and sounded the alert that the dismal state of public education threatened our very survival as a nation:

> Our nation is at risk. Our once unchallenged preeminence in commerce, industry, science, and technological innovation is being overtaken by competitors throughout the world. . . . The educational foundations of our society are presently being eroded by a rising tide of mediocrity that threatens our very future as a nation and a people. (p. 5)

Of course when the United States experienced unprecedented sustained economic growth in the 1990s while Asian economies languished, public schools received none of the credit. At some point, the following questions must be raised: How is it that the victims of an educational system that has been so deficient for half a century have continued to accomplish so much, and why is it that schools represent the fundamental problem in bad times but apparently contribute so little to the good?

It could be argued that there is much to celebrate when looking at the contemporary educational landscape. High school graduation rates have never been higher, a greater percentage of high school graduates are pursuing postsecondary education, more students are taking rigorous college-level courses in high school than ever before, and public approval for the quality of their local schools has risen 20% in the past two decades (Rose & Gallup, 2002). Yet once again the educational system has been deemed a failure, and new federal legislation has demanded that schools fix the problem by taking steps to ensure that no child is left behind.

The motivation behind NCLB legislation has been widely debated. Proponents portray the initiative as a sincere attempt to guarantee that every child, particularly poor and minority students, receives an education that leads to high levels of learning. Opponents contend the legislation is unrealistic and/or simplistic at best, or a thinly veiled attempt to dismantle the public system of education at worst. But regardless of the motivation, contemporary public schools in the United States are now being called upon to achieve a standard that goes far beyond the goals of any previous generation—high levels of learning for all students. Before addressing the issue, it may be beneficial to review the assumptions that have driven public schooling in the nation in the hope that a historical perspective can help clarify the current context.

Education for All: A Historical Perspective

Although the United States was the first nation to embrace the idea of free universal public education for all of its children, historically those children have been guaranteed only the right to attend school rather than the right to learn. In fact, the prevalent assumption that has driven public education throughout most of the history of the United States is that few students were capable of high levels of learning.

Thomas Jefferson, arguably one of the most liberal thinkers of his time, was one of the first Americans to call for universal public education. Jefferson linked education to the future of the new nation by arguing that "if a nation expects to be ignorant and free, in a state of civilization, it expects what never was and never will be" (1816). He made it clear, however, that the masses would never go beyond the most fundamental schooling. He proposed that all children in Virginia receive 3 years of free public education in reading, writing, and common arithmetic in a local school, but only the "boy of best genius" in each school would move on to one of the 20 grammar schools in the Commonwealth. After 1 or 2 years in the grammar school, "the best genius" among those students would be selected for another 4 or 5 years of education in Greek, Latin, geography, and the higher branches of mathematics while "the residue [was] dismissed." Jefferson explained that his plan was designed to ensure that 20 exceptional students would be "raked from the rubbish annually" and educated at the public expense. At the end of 6 years, 10 of those 20 would be dismissed from the public schools while the remaining 10, "chosen for the superiority of their parts and dispositions," would be sent on to William and Mary College to study science. For those who did not fall into the category of "genius," any education beyond a few years of elementary training was only possible for children of the "wealthier part of the people" who could afford it "at their own expense" (Jefferson, 1782).

Horace Mann, generally regarded as the father of the Common School Movement, argued that every child born had "the *absolute right"* to an education and that the state had the power and duty to tax everyone, not just those with children in school, to provide that education. Nevertheless, Mann stopped short of arguing that free public education should extend beyond grammar school. High school education was viewed as an option available only to those who could afford it. As late as the 1880s, America's most influential labor union staunchly opposed the public high school as "class education" for which only the beneficiaries should pay (Welter, 1963).

The idea that education for all should extend beyond elementary school came not from an egalitarian effort to ensure higher levels of learning for all students, but as a response to the immigration, urbanization, and industrialization that changed the face of the United States in the last decade of the 19th Century. Society faced new problems as many immigrants moved into the cities seeking jobs in factories, and schools were called upon to fill the social void. Ellwood Cubberly (1909), who later served as president of the National Education Association and Dean of Stanford University, argued that the first task of education was to address the needs of illiterate immigrants who lacked "self-reliance and initiative" and to "assimilate and amalgamate these people as part of our American race and to implant in their children so far as can be done, the Anglo-Saxon conception of righteousness, law and order, and popular government and to awaken in them a reverence for our democratic institutions" (p. 15).

The idea that public education should extend to secondary school was accompanied by the premise that the purpose of schooling for students at this level was no longer to be "common." In fact, the Common School concept of general education for all was criticized by leading educators as being based upon the "excessively democratic ideal that all are equal and our society is devoid of classes" (Cubberly, 1909, p. 57). Proponents of public high school argued that all students "cannot do and do not need the same education" (Leavitt, 1912, p. 2). This advocacy of differentiated schooling based upon such factors as a student's social and economic background, aptitude, needs, and interests offered a new definition of what constituted a democratic education.

This concept of differentiated schooling was quickly endorsed and implemented. The National Education Association (1910) applauded the recognition of "differences among children as to aptitudes, interests, economic resources, and prospective careers." The *Journal of Education* (1898) called it "the one great triumph of the new education" (p. 88).

Since the "new education" was based on the premise that students should be sorted into programs designed to meet their different abilities, educators began the search for instruments to assist with the sorting process. Psychologist Alfred Binet had been commissioned by the French government to design tests to differentiate between lazy or indifferent students and students with mental deficiencies so the latter could be removed from the public schools. In 1916 Lewis Terman of Stanford University extended Binet's initial work to include average and superior children with the creation of the Stanford-Binet test. It reported a student's ability as a number expressing the relation of the individual's mental age to his or her chronological age. The resulting intelligence quotient or IQ score provided schools with a single measure to assist in the sorting and selecting process.

When the United States entered World War I, tests assessing the intelligence of recruits were administered to hundreds of thousands of soldiers and then converted to IQ scores. The results suggested that the average mental age of Americans was 14, a finding that led many to conclude that most Americans were uneducable beyond high school. University presidents around the country used the results to argue that too many students were being admitted to college (Cremin, 1964). This complaint came at a time when only 16.4% of the American population aged 25 or older had earned a high school diploma and only 3.3% had attended college for 4 or more years (National Center for Education Statistics, 2000). Clearly, the idea that all students could learn at high levels was inconceivable to this generation of educators and to the public at large. Intelligence was something you were born with, not something you acquired.

The idea that a student's education should reflect his or her innate ability and socioeconomic status went largely unchallenged for the first three quarters of the 20th Century. Researchers continued to argue that differences in student achievement were not a function of the quality of schooling they received but merely reflected their aptitude and environment. A report titled "Equality in Educational Opportunity" published in 1966 concluded that schools had little influence on a child's achievement that was independent of the background and social context of that student (Coleman et al., 1966). Six years later another study reported that a student's achievement was primarily a function of his or her background, that schools did little to lessen the gap between more and less able students, and that there was little evidence to suggest school reform had any impact on student achievement (Jenks et al., 1972).

Gradually, however, researchers began to establish that what happens in schools does have a major impact on student achievement. Ron Edmonds, Larry Lezotte, Michael Rutter, and Wilbur Brookover were among the researchers who provided evidence that achievement among students from similar backgrounds varied significantly based on the practices of their schools. In his recent analysis of research conducted over a 35-year period, Robert Marzano (2003) concluded not only that schools have a significant impact upon student achievement, but also that "schools that are highly effective produce results that almost entirely overcome the effects of student backgrounds" (p. 7).

The effective school research challenged the long-standing belief that only those who had won the genetic lottery were capable of high levels of learning. Compelling evidence was presented to support two bold new premises: first, "all students can learn" and second, "schools control the factors necessary to assure student mastery of the core curriculum" (Lezotte, 2004).

The assertion that "all students can learn" became the rallying cry for schools throughout North America. Since the research had identified a "clear and focused mission" as one of the correlates of effective schools, schools and districts throughout the continent labored over the development and wordsmithing of their own mission statements. Although created in thousands of different school communities across the continent, these statements came to sound very much alike because they all reflected the premise that all children can learn. Yet, even as educators were congratulating themselves on their enlightened mission statements promising to help all students achieve at high levels, they often continued with traditional policies, programs, and procedures that virtually guaranteed all students would not learn. The longstanding belief that high levels of learning were reserved for the few and the structures that had been put in place to support that belief were not to be overcome by simply drafting a new mission statement.

Three Critical Questions

In our earlier books, *Professional Learning Communities at Work: Best Practices for Student Achievement* (1998) and *Getting Started: Reculturing Schools to Become Professional Learning Communities* (2002), we argue that when schools *truly* begin to align their practices with a commitment to learning for all, the educators within them begin to function as a Professional Learning Community (PLC). Working together collaboratively, the people in a PLC begin to focus on the three critical questions: Exactly what is it we want all students to learn? How will we know when each student has acquired the essential knowledge and skills? What happens in our school when a student does not learn?

Exactly What Is It We Want All Students to Learn?

Ask almost any teacher in North America if he or she believes all kids can learn, and it is almost guaranteed the teacher will answer in the affirmative. But ask that teacher if he or she believes all students can master calculus by the end of their freshman year of high school, and the answer will be an emphatic "no." Saying we believe all kids can learn is a pleasant affirmation, but it is only when teachers can articulate exactly what each student is expected to know and be able to do that the "learning for all" mission becomes possible.

Researchers found that in effective schools "each of the teachers in the school has a clear understanding of what the essential learner objectives are, grade by grade and course by course" (Lezotte, 2004). Marzano (2003) referred to this clarity of focus as a "guaranteed and viable curriculum." Doug Reeves (2004) describes the concept as "power standards." Regardless of the terminology, the premise of learning for all demands that each teacher knows exactly what every student is to accomplish as a result of each unit of instruction.

Unfortunately, many school districts that wrote new mission statements failed to initiate procedures to engage teachers in the clarification of the core curriculum. Some districts simply allowed each teacher to continue to determine what was significant and important for students to learn, resulting in wildly varying content and outcomes for students in the same grade level or course within a school. In other districts the central office staff developed voluminous curriculum guides and presented them to schools with the mistaken belief that teachers who had no involvement in the process would dutifully teach what they were told to teach. Some districts adopted textbook series and mandated that teachers not stray from them, and still others simply waited for the state or provincial governments to clarify the core curriculum. Despite the newly professed commitment to help all kids learn, districts typically failed to take adequate steps to ensure that every teacher was aware of and committed to the essential knowledge and skills students were to master.

How Will We Know When Each Student Has Acquired the Essential Knowledge and Skills?

If a school was truly committed to ensuring that every student mastered the intended outcomes of the core curriculum, it would be vigilant in its effort to assess each student's learning on a timely, ongoing basis. Unfortunately, once again, districts that adopted mission statements that promised "learning for all" typically failed to develop the procedures to answer the question, "Is each student learning?" Again, in some districts the nature and frequency of assessment was left to the discretion of individual teachers. More typically, districts used nationally normed assessments and focused on average scores in monitoring student achievement. This strategy is flawed in at least two ways. First, nationally normed tests are specifically designed to distribute students along a continuum of scores. The objective of these tests is not to assess an individual student's mastery of essential learning, but rather to differentiate between students with higher and lower scores. Second, average scores can hide the fact that some students are failing to achieve the intended outcomes. If a district contends that its mission is to help students learn "on average," focusing on nationally normed test results would be appropriate, but such assessments are incongruent with the mission of helping *each* student learn.

When states and provinces began to develop required exams for all of the students in their regions, the new exams typically did shift the focus from averages to individual student mastery. These mandated tests tended to be criterion-referenced assessments that asked if students had been able to achieve the designated standard of proficiency. While they represented an improvement over nationally normed tests, they failed to provide the timely feedback essential to learning. The information gleaned from state and provincial exams typically came too late in the year to be used to help students, most of whom had moved to the next grade.

Schools that operate as Professional Learning Communities use *formative* assessments on a frequent basis to ask, "Are the students learning and what steps must we take to address the needs of those who have not learned?" State and provincial assessments, on the other hand, typically represent *summative* assessments that ask, "Did the students learn what they were supposed to have learned by the designated deadline?" Rick Stiggins differentiates between formative and summative assessment by clarifying that the former is "assessment *for* learning" while the latter is "assessment *of* learning" (2002). One is used on an ongoing basis to monitor individual student learning and to impact instructional practice so that all students master intended outcomes. The other is used to assign a designation and, quite often, punitive consequences for students who fail to meet the standard. The difference between a formative and summative assessment has also been described as the difference between a physical examination and an autopsy. The intent of one is to diagnose and prescribe the appropriate intervention; the intent of the other is to explain why the patient (or student) failed to make it. PLCs prefer physicals to autopsies.

What Happens in our School When a Student Does Not Learn?

Marzano (2003) has described three different levels of curriculum. The first is the intended curriculum—what we intend for each student to learn. The second is the implemented curriculum—what is actually taught. The third is the attained curriculum—what students actually learn. A school that is truly committed to learning for all would take steps to address all three levels. Every teacher would be clear on what students are to learn. Procedures would be in place to guarantee that every student has access to that intended learning in his or her classroom. Each student's attainment of the intended outcomes would be carefully monitored. But even with all this in place, if schools are to consider the mission of learning for all as a genuine pledge rather than politically correct hyperbole, they must turn their attention to a third critical question: What happens in our school when a student does not learn?

In our earlier work we have focused primarily on the steps schools can take to create the collaborative culture in which teachers work together in teams as part of a continuous improvement process that clarifies outcomes, assesses student learning, and assists teachers in developing new ideas and strategies to raise current levels of student achievement. This book is intended to address the third critical question facing schools that hope to become Professional Learning Communities: What happens in our school when a student does not learn? We consider this question to be the fork in the road— the one question more than any other that will demonstrate a school's commitment to learning for all students and its progress on the road to becoming a PLC.

The NCLB legislation has added a new dimension to the discussion about what happens when students do not learn. Whereas the premise that "all kids can learn" is a relatively new concept in the history of education, NCLB has now shifted the premise to "all kids will learn—or else." The legislation threatens schools and the educators within them with escalating sanctions if they fail to meet newly imposed standards. The rationale behind this approach suggests that educators have always known how to help all kids learn but have been too disinterested in the welfare of their students or too lazy to put forth the necessary effort. Fear is needed to provide the necessary motivation—either perform or risk closing your school and/or losing your job.

We believe this premise is fundamentally flawed. First, we believe that teachers, in general, have the best interests of their students at heart and are willing to work very, very hard in the effort to help all students be successful. In fact, we contend that there are few, if any, occupations in which people work harder than teachers. Second, the idea that people can be threatened or coerced into higher performance runs contrary to what is universally recognized as best practice for leading organizations. Fear may produce some short-term efforts, but it is ineffective at generating the sustained motivation necessary to transform a school into a PLC. The NCLB threat to continue the beatings until morale improves seems far more likely to drive educators out of the profession and potential educators into other more satisfying fields than to create the energy and enthusiasm for the difficult work at hand.

Thus, we are not apologists for NCLB, and in fact, we are deeply disturbed by many of the specific provisions of the act. We do, however, acknowledge the need for schools to move beyond pious mission statements pledging learning for all and to begin the systematic effort to create procedures, policies, and programs that are aligned with that purpose.

Our objective in writing this book is *not* to help schools raise test scores and avoid sanctions. Our purpose is twofold. First, we hope to persuade educators that we should take our mission statements literally. We should indeed promote high levels of learning for every child entrusted to us, not because of legislation or fear of sanctions, but because we have a moral and ethical imperative to do so. We can no longer claim that our efforts have no impact on the learning of our students. Second, it is possible to help more students succeed at higher levels than ever before *if* we are willing to change many of our assumptions and practices, most of which draw their origins from earlier times when education was intended to serve a far different purpose. This book rests upon the conviction that test scores will take care of themselves if educators commit to ensuring that each student masters essential skills and concepts in every unit of instruction, align their practices and resources toward that purpose, and discontinue many traditional practices that do not serve that purpose.

In short, we hope both to challenge educators to reflect upon the current practices in their schools and classrooms and to offer specific suggestions as to how they might better meet the daunting but vitally important challenge of helping all students learn at high levels.

Chapter 2

How Do We Respond When Kids Don't Learn?

"When you start with an honest and diligent effort to determine the truth of the situation, the right decisions often become self-evident. . . . You absolutely cannot make a series of good decisions without first confronting the brutal facts."

—Jim Collins, 2001, p. 70

"Students' learning experiences . . . with weak teaching cultures are akin to an instructional lottery, in which their learning opportunities depend heavily on which teachers they draw, from class to class and year to year."

—Milbrey McLaughlin & Joan Talbert, 2001, p. 64

Often in our workshops we ask participants to consider four different sample schools whose staffs would endorse the statement that "all kids can learn." Upon closer examination, however, it becomes apparent that each school is driven by very different assumptions and, because of those differing assumptions, the schools would respond to a student who was not learning in very different ways. Participants in the workshop are asked to review the assumptions, and then predict how each school would respond when a student experiences academic difficulty. The description of the four schools is presented below.

The Charles Darwin School

"We believe all kids can learn . . . based on their ability."

We believe that all students can learn, but the extent of their learning is determined by their innate ability or aptitude. This aptitude is relatively fixed, and as teachers we have little influence over the extent of student learning. It is our job to create multiple programs or tracks that address the different abilities of students and then guide students to the appropriate program. This ensures that students have access to the proper curriculum and an optimum opportunity to master material appropriate to their ability.

The Pontius Pilate School

"We believe all kids can learn . . . if they take advantage of the opportunity we give them to learn."

We believe that all students can learn if they elect to put forth the necessary effort. It is our job to provide all students with an opportunity to learn, and we fulfill our responsibility when we attempt to present lessons that are both clear and engaging. In the final analysis, however, while it is our job to teach, it is the student's job to learn. We should invite students to learn, but if they elect not to do so, we must hold them accountable for their decisions.

The Chicago Cub Fan School

"We believe all kids can learn . . . something, and we will help all students experience academic growth in a warm and nurturing environment."

We believe that all students can learn and that it is our responsibility to help all students demonstrate some growth as a result of their experience with us. The extent of the growth will be determined by a combination of the student's innate ability and effort. Although we have little impact on those factors, we can encourage all students to learn as much as possible and we can and will create an environment that fosters their sense of well-being and self-esteem.

The Henry Higgins School

"We believe all kids can learn . . . and we will work to help all students achieve high standards of learning."

We believe that all students can and must learn at relatively high levels of achievement. We are confident that students can master challenging academic material with our support and help. We establish standards all students are expected to achieve, and we continue to work with them until they have done so.

Participants in the workshop typically have very little trouble predicting the responses of the various schools. The Charles Darwin School will respond to a student who is not learning by recommending that the student be placed in a less rigorous program. If a student is experiencing difficulty in getting over the proficiency bar that has been established in a course, the school responds by lowering the bar.

The Pontius Pilate School holds the student accountable for not doing what was necessary to learn by failing the student. The hope is that a student who suffers the logical consequences of irresponsibility (that is, failure) will learn the error of his or her ways and become more motivated in the future.

The Chicago Cub Fan School adjusts the goals for individual students within the course or grade level, assuming that low-performing students lack the ability, motivation, or developmental readiness to learn at high levels. The priority in the school becomes ensuring students feel good rather than ensuring that they have learned.

The Henry Higgins School calls upon staff to devote extra time to students who experience difficulty in learning and to continue to seek new strategies until every student has achieved the intended academic goals. Teachers never give up and simply work harder at meeting the needs of individual students.

We then ask participants to identify which of the four schools they believe is most prevalent in North America today. We have asked this question of tens of thousands of educators all across the continent and found invariably consistent responses. Most participants divide themselves fairly equally among the Darwin, Pilate, and Cub Fan schools. A few lonely souls will contend that most schools operate according to Henry Higgins assumptions. Often participants will suggest that the response varies according to the grade level of the school—elementary schools tend to operate according to Cub Fan principles while high schools may be more prone to embrace Darwin principles.

Once everyone has had the chance to weigh in on the debate, we ask this question: "Is it not true that in the real world of schools in North America today, we have *all four* of these responses occurring in the same school at the same time?" In one classroom where a student is struggling, the teacher is likely to call for the student to be placed in a different, less rigorous program. In a classroom down the hall, another student with similar difficulty will remain in the class and receive a failing grade. In yet another classroom, the teacher begins to make concessions to the student's perceived deficiencies and adjusts his or her academic goals for the student. Finally, in even the lowest-performing schools, there are those heroic teachers who continue to exert extraordinary effort in their quest to help all students achieve at high levels. Every time we have posed this question, the audience of experienced educators has agreed: Students in the same school who experience difficulty in learning will be subject to very different responses based upon the beliefs and practices of individual teachers.

We contend that a school truly committed to the concept of learning for each student will stop subjecting students to a haphazard, random, *de facto* educational lottery program when they struggle academically. It will stop leaving the critical question, "How will we respond when a student is not learning?" to the discretion of each teacher. It will instead develop consistent, systematic procedures that ensure each student is guaranteed additional time and support when needed. In fact, until the staff of a school begins to respond to students communally rather than as individuals, the school will never become a Professional Learning Community.

A Key Shift in Assumptions: Learning as the Constant, Time and Support as Variables

Here is a typical scenario that plays out daily in traditional schools. A teacher has diligently studied state and district curriculum guides to determine the essential knowledge and skills every student is to acquire as a result of the next unit. She teaches the unit according to the best of her ability and assesses each student's learning at its conclusion. The results make it evident that some students have not mastered the essential outcomes. On the one hand the teacher would like to take the time to help those students. On the other hand she feels compelled to move forward in order to cover the course content. If the teacher uses instructional time to assist those who have not learned, the needs of students who have mastered the content are not being met; if the teacher pushes on with new concepts, struggling students are likely to fall farther behind.

This commonplace occurrence typically forces teachers and students to enter into an implicit, unstated contract. In effect, the teacher begins the unit saying:

> "Kids, there is a very important concept in this unit we are about to begin, and I really want all of you to learn it. But I can only devote 3 weeks to this concept, and then we have to push on to cover all the other concepts I am supposed to teach you this year. The schedule limits us to 50 minutes a day, and I can't make it 55 minutes. So, during this unit, time to learn will be a constant: you all will have 50 minutes a day for 3 weeks. When it comes to giving you individual attention and support, I'll do the best I can. But I can't

spend a lot of class time helping a few of you who are having difficulty if the rest of the kids have learned it. That is not fair to those students. So, in effect, you will all have essentially the same amount of support during this unit."

When time and support are regarded as constants, learning will be the variable no matter how hard an individual teacher may work. Some students, probably most students, will learn, and some will not. Educators regret that fact, but they understand that is how school operates.

A Professional Learning Community operates from a very different premise. A teacher in a PLC begins the unit by advising students of an *essential* outcome, an outcome so important, so significant, that every student *must* achieve it. Learning will be the constant. In this situation, it is imperative that time and support become variables. Some students will require more time to learn, and so the school will develop strategies to provide students with that time during the school day. Some students will require more support for learning. They may never learn the concept in the classroom setting, and so the school will develop systems to provide them with small-group or one-on-one tutorials until they have achieved mastery. Rather than placing responsibility for student learning solely on the back of overburdened classroom teachers, the school will develop a *collective* response to assist classroom teachers by giving students extra time and extra support. Teachers working in isolated classrooms will be unable to implement the most effective strategies to help all students learn at high levels; those strategies will require the cooperation of the school as a whole.

Providing Time and Support

The rest of this book will illustrate how this system of time and support for students can work in the real world of schools; however, a few caveats are in order. First, the examples we provide come from schools that have been at work in building their system of response for a number of years. The examples are comprehensive, but it is important that readers understand these systems did not suddenly emerge fully formed. The process was messy and nonlinear as the schools learned through trial and error what worked and what did not work. Many of the steps in the system of response were developed only when earlier steps failed to accomplish all that was hoped for when they were implemented.

Second, the examples are offered as illustrations of what schools can accomplish when staff members work together to consider the question, "What happens in our school when students do not learn?" They are not intended to serve as models for other schools to transplant. *Each staff must develop its own plan for meeting the needs of students in their unique school.* Not every program presented in the following chapters will be desirable or even possible for every school in every state or province. Avoid the temptation to simply dismiss the example with a cursory, "We can't do that here," and accept the challenge of working with colleagues to identify alternatives that can work in your setting.

Third, the idea that schools can provide students with additional time and support relies more on determination and will than on additional resources. We understand the budgetary constraints schools are facing and recognize the futility in offering ideas for improvement that demand significant additional expenditures. We are convinced that support systems can be provided within existing resources because we have done it. It is not imperative to have a windfall of additional funding to implement these ideas, but it is imperative that staff members demonstrate a willingness to change some traditional assumptions, practices, roles, and responsibilities.

Finally, no system of intervention will ever compensate for bad teaching. A school that focuses exclusively on responding to students who are having difficulty without also developing the capacity of every administrator and teacher to become more effective will fail to become a Professional Learning Community. The most important resource in every school will continue to be the professionals within it. Implementing procedures to monitor each student's learning on a timely basis and creating systems of intervention to assist students who need additional time and support are necessary steps in becoming a PLC, but they are not sufficient. The professionals within the school will also be called upon to build a collaborative culture, engage in collective inquiry regarding matters that impact student learning, participate in action research, create continuous improvement processes, and help each other monitor and improve upon results. They will do more than voice the belief that all students can learn; they will act on that belief. They will create a shared vision of the school they must create in order to help all students learn. They will identify and honor collective commitments clarifying what they are prepared to do to move their school toward that shared vision.

Our earlier books and videos focus primarily on providing educators with the time, support, and strategies to enhance their professional practice. This book focuses primarily on providing time, support, and strategies to assist students; however, the importance of building the capacity of a staff to function as a PLC cannot be overemphasized and must not be overlooked. As Roland Barth (2001) concluded:

> Ultimately there are two kinds of schools: learning-enriched schools and learning-impoverished schools. I've yet to see a school where the learning curves of the youngsters are off the chart upward while the learning curves of the adults are off the chart downward, or a school where the learning curves of the adults were steep upward and those of the students were not. Teachers and students go hand in hand as learners—or they don't go at all. (p. 23)

A Scenario: A Mission Without a Plan

The mother of Johnny Jones is anxious but hopeful as the first day of high school approaches for her son. Johnny had become increasingly indifferent toward school over the past several years, but she is hopeful that something or someone will spark his interest in his high school, a school with the motto of "Success for Every Student."

During the first 2 months of school, she makes several efforts to engage Johnny in conversation about his freshman year, hoping to get some sense of how he is enjoying school and how he is doing academically. Johnny, however, is generally uncommunicative beyond a terse assurance that everything at school is "fine."

Finally, desperate for information, Mrs. Jones calls Johnny's counselor at school and expresses concern that 8 weeks have gone by and she has received no information on her son's progress. The counselor reassures her that at this school, "no news is good news." She explains that teachers are required to send a progress report to the parents of any student who is failing their class, and since Johnny's mother had not received any progress reports, "Johnny must be doing fine." She also explains that the semester is divided into two 9-week grading periods. At the end of the 9 weeks, teachers will be given several days to calculate and report grades and data processing will require 2 days to print report cards and mail them to parents. The counselor assures Mrs. Jones that when Johnny gets his report card in the eleventh week of the 18-week semester, they will have a much better picture regarding his achievement. She suggests that Mrs. Jones call her again when reports cards are issued.

Three weeks later when the report card arrives, Mrs. Jones discovers her son has received the grade of D in three of his core classes. She dutifully contacts each teacher to get advice on what she can do to help her son improve his performance. The algebra teacher advises her that Johnny is not "algebra ready" and seems to lack the prerequisite skills for success in the course. He advises that Johnny should be placed in a Pre-Algebra class to work on his skills and offers to initiate the schedule change.

The World History teacher advises Mrs. Jones that Johnny failed to meet the deadline on several assignments, that he does not accept work that is turned in after the deadline, and that the resulting zeros lowered Johnny's grade to a D. The teacher explains that while it is his job to teach, it is not his job to make sure that Johnny does his homework. He advises Mrs. Jones that Johnny must learn to accept responsibility for himself. He suggests that she encourage Johnny to do his homework each night; however, she must let Johnny find his own solution to his problems in World History rather than try to solve his problems for him.

Johnny's English teacher advises Mrs. Jones that Johnny lacked confidence in his ability to write and failed to turn in several assignments. She attempted to give him alternative methods to express himself, such as turning in a collage of pictures to communicate his emotions and thoughts, but he did not complete those assignments either. She is convinced that Johnny's problem is rooted in a lack of self-esteem, and she advises Mrs. Jones to reassure her son that he is a very special young man each day.

Unfortunately, Johnny's academic performance in the second semester declined still further. At the end of the semester he had failed three classes and his counselor advised Mrs. Jones that perhaps Johnny should be considered for special education.

How did this school respond when Johnny experienced academic difficulty? In fact, the *school* never responds to Johnny. The issue of what to do about Johnny was left to the discretion of individual teachers, who were free to respond in very different ways. Instead of working together to develop a systematic plan of intervention to meet the needs of students who were struggling, the school abdicated its collective responsibility and turned the matter over to each teacher to resolve.

Unfortunately, this situation represents the norm in most schools. In schools throughout North America, teachers begin the year with the sincere hope that they will be able to help all of their students learn the most essential knowledge and skills of their grade levels or courses. They work very, very hard to achieve this goal of learning for all. Yet, by the third or fourth week of school, it becomes evident that some students are not learning. This finding never comes as a surprise. Although it happens each year, schools that proclaim their mission is to ensure learning for all have no plan or strategy for responding to the inevitable moment when a student is not learning.

Consider the following analogy: You enter a Starbucks shop at 7:00 a.m. secure in the knowledge that Starbucks has a well-defined and well-understood mission—selling overpriced coffee in a comfortable environment. On this particular morning, however, you discover that this Starbucks is out of coffee. Certainly this would strike you as odd since a Starbucks without coffee cannot fulfill its fundamental mission. You would question why the staff had not developed a plan both to monitor the quantity of coffee in the restaurant and to respond in a timely and systematic way whenever those quantities dropped to a certain level. The absence of a response plan would strike you as extremely peculiar and as incongruous with the mission of Starbucks.

Yet, throughout North America, schools that pledge their allegiance to the mission of learning for all have no plan for responding when a student is not learning. One of the key messages of this book is that a Professional Learning Community acknowledges the incongruity between a proposed commitment to learning for all and the absence of a coordinated strategy to respond when students do not learn. The staff addresses this discrepancy by designing systems and processes to ensure that students who experience difficulty receive additional time and support for their learning—regardless of who their teacher might be. Our investigation of how those systems and processes might operate begins in the next chapter.

Chapter 3

A High School's Collective Response When Kids Don't Learn: Adlai Stevenson High School

"In the factory model of schooling, quality was the variable; time was the constant. Students were given a set amount of work to do in a set period of time, then graded on the quality of what was accomplished. We held time constant, and allowed quality to vary. We must turn that on its head: Hold the quality of the work constant, and allow time to vary. We must realize we have the power to achieve a common curriculum by uncommon means."

—Robert Cole & Phillip Schlechty, 1993, p. 10

"Students simply cannot fall through the cracks here. We have too many systems in place to monitor their academic progress and general well-being and too many concerned adults involved in the implementation of those systems. Kids learn quickly that if they do not perform they will be answering to a coordinated team of staff members who will insist they put in extra time and get the help necessary to succeed."

—Dan Galloway, Principal, Adlai Stevenson High School

Adlai Stevenson High School in suburban Chicago is one of three schools in the nation to receive the United States Department of Education Blue Ribbon award on four separate occasions—an accomplishment which means that the school has continuously increased student achievement for two decades. It is one of the first comprehensive high schools in America to be designated "A New American High School" as a model of successful school reform and has been described as "an undeniably world-class school" (Schmoker, 2001). Yet everything described in the Johnny Jones scenario in chapter 2 came directly from Stevenson High School in the early 1980s. The motto of the school was "Success for Every Student," and the faculty was characterized by an exceptional work ethic. Many students flourished in the Stevenson environment; but, despite all of the faculty's hard work, many other students were unsuccessful. More than 25% of the student body had been relegated to remedial curricular tracks and, at the end of each semester, teachers were recommending that hundreds of students be transferred to a lower track. The failure rate topped 30%, and the annual number of out-of-school suspensions as a percentage of the student body had risen to over 75%.

In 1983 the school began a process to investigate steps that might be taken to address the needs of students who were not being successful. The process included building shared knowledge about the current reality of the school and then engaging faculty, parents, and students in dialogue about the reasons more students were not being successful. The causes they identified could probably apply to most high schools.

Teacher concerns included:

- **The middle schools are not providing us with enough information on incoming freshmen.** Students were placed into the Stevenson curriculum solely on the basis of their performance on a single nationally normed test administered to them in eighth grade. A local percentile ranking was established for each member of the incoming class and students were then assigned into one of the high school's five curriculum tracks on the basis of their rank. Placement was based upon rigid caps and quotas. Only 10% of the incoming students could qualify for the most rigorous track (the honors program) while 25% were automatically relegated to the two remedial tracks (the modified and basic programs). High school teachers had no access to information regarding the strengths and weaknesses of a particular student. All that was available to a teacher who wanted to explore background information on a student was the student's grades from middle school, immunization record, and local percentile ranking from the nationally normed test. Teachers complained that they were working in the dark.

- **Incoming students lack study skills and good work habits.** There was widespread concern among the high school faculty that many incoming freshmen had not learned how to study. They questioned the rigor of the middle schools and were convinced that many students were unprepared and/or unwilling to meet the reasonable work demands in their courses.

- **Consequences for failure are inadequate and there are no incentives for good academic performance.** It was evident to teachers that many students were unaffected by a failing grade and were, in fact, quite willing to fail rather than do what was necessary to succeed. Teachers called for more dire consequences for failure and meaningful incentives to reward students who were being successful.

Parents had a different perspective on the reasons why students were unsuccessful at Stevenson. The phrase they used over and over again to describe the problem was this: "Stevenson lets students fall through the cracks." They criticized the school both for its inability to identify a student who was having difficulty until it was too late, and for its tendency to seek a solution by moving students to lower tracks. One tearful mother recounted that she had sent her son to Stevenson with high hopes for his success, but week after week went by with no feedback from the school. Finally, in the eleventh week of the semester she received his report card and found that he had received three grades of D. As she explained it:

> "Doesn't anyone at Stevenson understand the implications of your failure to keep parents informed about the progress of our students? My son will never be admitted to the leading public university in our state because 50% of his grade in his first semester of high school has been locked in as a D. He no longer has access to a

number of opportunities and options that are available to successful students. Yet no one in the school had the courtesy to let me know he was having difficulty. How do you expect parents to be partners in the education of their children if you keep us in the dark until it is too late?"

Students presented yet another explanation for their lack of success. Many students, particularly those in the remedial tracks, felt no connection with their school. High school was something to be endured rather than enjoyed. They regarded class work as boring and questioned whether anyone at the school really took an interest in them as individuals.

If the purpose of school is simply to give students the *opportunity* to learn, Stevenson was fulfilling its purpose in the early 1980s. Many of its students were achieving at very high levels, and the school could point to them as evidence that the problem was not with the school, but with the inability or unwillingness of some students to put forth the effort to learn. But, to the enduring credit of Stevenson's wonderful faculty, they did not settle for giving students the chance to learn. Instead, they began a systematic effort to better meet the needs of all students so that the school's promise of "success for all" might be a reality rather than a slogan.

Pre-Enrollment Initiatives

When the Stevenson staff took time to analyze the current reality of the school, it became evident that the school needed to become more proactive in identifying students who would need additional support in order to be successful in high school. As a result of that finding, several new programs and procedures were initiated.

Placement by Proficiency Rather Than by Caps and Quotas

Although Stevenson claimed to embrace the idea of "success for all," its placement procedures reflected the selecting and sorting mentality upon which schools had been built earlier in the century. The nationally normed test administered to students for their placement into the high school was used not to assess the proficiency of individual students in essential areas of learning, but rather to establish a continuum of scores for assigning students into programs according to the bell-shaped curve. A score that might qualify a student for the regular college preparatory program one year could relegate a student to a remedial program the next. It was not the score that mattered in placing a student: it was the student's rank within the incoming class that determined his or her placement. Furthermore, the results from the nationally normed test did not provide teachers with an assessment of an individual student's mastery of essential knowledge and skills. Teachers had no relevant information regarding the academic achievement of the students assigned to their classes.

Ultimately, the staff recognized the incongruity between a mission statement that promised to help all students reach high levels of achievement and a school structure designed to sort and select students according to the bell-shaped curve. Working in partnership with teachers from the six middle schools, they began the exploration of the first critical question of a PLC: What is it we want all students to learn? Within a few months teachers were able to clarify what every student leaving eighth grade was expected to know and be able to do in the areas of reading, writing, mathematics, and foreign languages.

The high school and middle school teachers then turned their attention to the second critical question: How will we know if each student has achieved the intended outcomes by the end of eighth grade? State assessments had not yet been developed, so the middle school and the high school teachers worked together to develop criterion-referenced proficiency tests to answer that question. These proficiency tests became the new basis for placing students into Stevenson's newly designed program.

The five different ability levels were collapsed into three. A standard proficiency score was established based on the recommendation of the teachers who had developed the test, and students were advised that all those who reached that standard in a given area of the test would be invited into the honors program—a program specifically designed to help students earn college credits while still in high school. A second score was established as the qualifying standard for entry into the college-preparatory program—a program designed to provide students with a solid, rigorous liberal arts curriculum that would prepare them for success in higher education. Placement was by area rather than by track; that is, a student who qualified for honors mathematics might be recommended for the college preparatory English program.

Students who were unable to achieve the prerequisite score for either the honors or college preparatory curriculum were recommended for the modified program. This program, however, was designed to be far different than the remedial programs that preceded it. Students assigned to those earlier programs had languished there for 4 years. There was virtually no opportunity for upward mobility into higher-level curriculum. The new structure, however, limited modified courses to the freshman and sophomore years. Juniors and seniors would have only two levels available to them—college preparatory and honors. This change redefined the entire purpose of the modified program. No longer was it to serve as a 4-year holding pen; now it was to serve as a 2-year launching pad that accelerated student learning so that every student would have access to college preparatory curriculum in their final 2 years. Juniors and seniors who pursued technical or vocational programs were now expected to complete the same English, math, science, and social studies courses as their college-bound classmates.

The proficiency tests were not used as a barrier to student aspirations. If students or parents were disappointed with the recommended placement, students were given multiple opportunities to demonstrate proficiency on different forms of the placement test during the second semester of eighth grade. A summer program was offered for students who sought tutoring in order to improve their placement. And in the final analysis, if the student or parent persisted in seeking the higher placement despite the school's recommendation, the student would be enrolled in the more advanced course and given 6 weeks to demonstrate that he or she was capable of meeting its standards.

With the administration of these new proficiency tests to eighth graders, high school teachers were able to identify the particular strengths and weaknesses of each student entering their classroom as freshmen. Junior high school teachers were provided with an analysis of the proficiency of their graduates in each of the skills assessed on the new tests. This vital information enabled them to identify areas of the curriculum that needed more attention. The results from these placement tests over the two decades they have been administered have been invaluable in helping teachers at both levels become more skilled at meeting the needs of their students.

Counselor Watch

The Stevenson faculty recognized that it was not always academic deficiency that led students to struggle in high school. Some students had plenty of ability but little motivation. Others faced emotional difficulties or family problems that impacted their achievement. Staff members were concerned that they did not have sufficient information to address the various needs of their students. The Counselor Watch program was created to address this problem.

Every January, Stevenson counselors ask the principal of each of the middle schools that send their graduates to Stevenson to complete a Counselor Watch Referral Sheet for any student who meets the criteria for the program—poor academic progress, personal or family problems, poor attendance, peer relationship issues, low self-esteem, or chronic underachievement. In effect, Stevenson asks the staff of each middle school, "Which students will need our help the most?"

In April, Stevenson counselors visit every middle school to review the referral sheets with the middle school principal, counselor, social worker, and nurse. These meetings not only clarify and elaborate upon the concerns the middle school staff may have regarding a student, but also identify the interventions and support the student will require in entering high school. Students are identified for specific programs and services months before they ever enter the high school. Rather than waiting for the student to experience frustration and failure before responding to the situation, the school assumes a proactive stance that provides students with intervention and support services designed to promote their immediate success in high school.

Proactive Student Registration

Each February, Stevenson counselors travel to the middle schools to meet with individual eighth-grade students and their parents to register students for their freshman classes. Counselors use this opportunity to foster an expectation of achievement and participation. All students are asked to identify three goals they hope to achieve during their freshmen year, as well as three co-curricular activities they may want to do. These conversations reveal a great deal about student dispositions toward their upcoming high school experience and begin the personal connection between counselors and students.

Summer Study Skills Course

Stevenson created a special summer school course to address the lack of study skills of many incoming freshmen. This course, "Survival Skills for High School," was designed to teach students how to take notes, annotate their reading, use a planner to organize their time and materials, read for comprehension, set goals, and communicate effectively. Parents of any student who received two or more grades of D in middle school are specifically contacted by Stevenson counselors and urged to enroll their son or daughter in this summer program. The course is taught by a Stevenson teacher who has both a talent and interest in working with students who have a history of achieving below their academic potential. The course runs for

4 hours each day for 4 weeks each summer, and students who complete the course receive one elective credit.

The initial response to this program was underwhelming. After reviewing the situation, Stevenson staff found that the course faced two major obstacles. First, like all of the summer school courses offered by the school, it was scheduled at the same time as many of the athletic camps being offered at the high school. Students were forced to make a choice between a summer school course or football, basketball, volleyball, and soccer camps—and summer school was losing that competition. So the decision was made to stop forcing students to make that choice. Coaches were told that athletic camps could not be offered while summer school was in session. Since classes were scheduled from 8:00 a.m. until noon for 8 weeks, most coaches simply moved their camps to the afternoon to give students the opportunity to take advantage of both programs.

The second obstacle was more problematic. North American students have been conditioned to regard summer school as punitive. For years they have heard, "You had better improve your grades or we will force you to go to summer school." So when parents suggested the "Survival Skills for High School" course to their sons and daughters, most students were adamantly opposed to enrolling. They wanted nothing to do with the program because of the perceived social stigma of attending summer school.

Stevenson attacked this problem by expanding its summer school options in every department and beginning a concentrated effort to convince parents that every incoming freshman would benefit from enrolling in a summer school course. At every meeting with parents of eighth graders, the principal and counselors pointed out how much more comfortable students would be on the first day of high school if they had already learned their way around the building, had met students from other middle schools, had discovered what the homework load was like in a high school class, and had earned a credit because of enrolling in a summer school course. When counselors met with parents to register students for their freshman courses, they also brought registration materials for the summer program. Because the district had a policy that summer school had to be revenue neutral, tuition was charged for all summer programs; however, a Community Foundation was established to pay the tuition of any student who needed financial assistance. Attending summer school lost its stigma, and today at Stevenson, over 80% of every entering freshman class enrolls in a summer school course.

The Good Friend Program

The Counselor Watch process might also result in a student being recommended for the Good Friend Program. This program provides additional encouragement, support, and attention to students who are experiencing problems that might impact their school performance. Prior to the first day of school, counselors link a student with an individual teacher who agrees to take a special interest in the student. The teacher pledges to make a sustained effort to connect with the student, to discover the student's concerns and interests, and to establish a positive personal relationship. The Good Friend teacher advises both the student regarding the difficulty he or she may be experiencing and the counselor regarding the best ways to assist the student. Students are unaware that they have been identified for the program or that they are the beneficiaries of this extra effort to assist them.

Counselor Check-In Program

Students identified for the Counselor Check-In Program during the Counselor Watch discussions are scheduled to meet individually with their counselors on a weekly basis for at least the first 6 weeks of the school year. During these private conversations, the counselor monitors the academic progress and emotional well-being of the student and attempts to help the student find solutions to any problems he or she may be experiencing.

Assisting All Students With the Transition to High School

A second initiative identified by the Stevenson staff fell into the broad category of providing greater support for all incoming students as they made the transition into high school. They were able to develop a comprehensive support system by collectively considering the questions, "What can we do to promote the academic success of every entering student, and what steps can we take to help each student feel personally connected to people and programs in our schools?"

Freshman Orientation Day

When staff members asked juniors and seniors to reflect on the hardest thing about the first day of high school, a consistent response was how self-conscious they felt trying to find their way around the building in the presence of older students. They explained it was difficult to be "cool" when they were obviously lost, much to the amusement of other students.

Stevenson addressed this problem by scheduling freshmen to attend school one day earlier than the rest of the student body. A portion of the day was spent in a general orientation to the school that included tours of the building. Students also followed an abbreviated schedule that allowed them to find their way from class to class and to meet their teachers. The day ended with a pep rally and welcome party sponsored by the Parent Association. The Student Council took the lead in Freshman Orientation, and selected juniors and seniors led tours, assisted students, and answered questions. When the rest of the student body arrived the next day, the inevitable anxiety that freshmen feel as they begin high school had been diminished considerably.

Freshman Advisory Program

The daily schedule for freshmen was designed so that all freshmen would meet with their faculty advisor 4 days each week for 25 minutes. The advisor was not responsible for providing instruction but instead was asked to create an environment where students could relax, get to know one another, and have their questions answered. The advisor was also responsible for monitoring the academic achievement of each student and counseling individual students regarding any difficulties they were experiencing.

Because all of the students assigned to an advisor had the same counselor, the counselor would attend the advisory 1 day each week to check in on each student and to assist with any difficulties a student might be experiencing. This weekly visit served a variety of purposes. Counselors were able to build relationships with their new students as they came to know each student as an individual. Conversations went beyond academic progress to include the student's involvement in co-curricular activities, interests, hobbies, and goals for high school. Counselors were able to share the most pertinent information with small groups of freshmen in a setting that encouraged students to ask questions and seek clarification. Counselors were assured weekly contact with each of their freshmen and could schedule a more private meeting with any student who might need extra help. Thus, the Freshman Advisory Program gave each incoming student sustained contact and a personal relationship with two caring adults: an advisor and a counselor.

Freshman Mentor Program (FMP)

Assisting each faculty advisor were five upperclassmen mentors who met with their 25 freshmen each day during the advisory period. The upperclassmen divided the 25 students among themselves, with each assuming responsibility for 5 freshmen. The mentor's job was to do whatever was necessary to help his or her 5 students become successful at Stevenson. Within the first week of school, all freshmen were required to pass a test on the school rulebook; mentors tutored them on the rules until each freshman was able to pass. By the fourth week of school, all freshmen were required to solidify their academic, social, and participation goals for their 4 years of high school, and their mentor guided them through that process. Most importantly, every freshman knew that he or she had a Big Brother or Big Sister to turn to each day for help with questions that could range from "How do I ask a girl to Homecoming?" to "What is the best way to study for final exams?"

Participation in Co-Curricular Programs

Stevenson offered a wide array of co-curricular programs to its students—athletics, clubs, fine arts, community service— but surveys of students revealed that many were electing not to participate. When staff reviewed research that demonstrated students who become involved in school activities experience greater satisfaction with school and higher academic achievement than those who do not, they concluded that Stevenson should do a better job of engaging incoming students in the co-curricular program. A Co-Curricular Handbook was created to describe each activity and any requirements for participation. A Co-Curricular Fair was scheduled to give freshmen information on every program and to answer any questions the students or parents might have about that program. Students who indicated an interest in a particular program were sent a letter by the sponsor urging them to join and advising them of procedures for doing so. Finally, when counselors met with incoming freshmen and parents to register students for courses, they also registered the students for a co-curricular activity.

The school schedule was adjusted to provide an activity period during the school day each month. Club sponsors could use that period to schedule meetings with members. A student who was intent on finding a co-curricular program that made no demands on his or her time outside of the school day could join a program that only met during the activity period, but few chose that option. The school created the expectation that every student needed to belong to something—a team, a cast, an ensemble, or a club—and that no one would remain on the periphery throughout their high school years.

Frequent Monitoring of Student Progress

When Stevenson staff compared the practices of their school to research findings on the characteristics of highly effective schools, it became evident that procedures used for reporting student progress were problematic. Although the research called for frequent monitoring of student learning and strong partnerships with parents, Stevenson grading practices made it impossible for either the school or parents to get an overview of a student's academic performance until the eleventh week of the semester. The school could not respond to students on a timely basis and parents were being kept in the dark.

Stevenson addressed this discrepancy by creating a faculty task force and presenting its members with the charge to develop reporting procedures that reflected best practice and were more aligned with the school's mission of success for all. After examining the research, looking at the practices of other schools, and investigating the potential of technology to assist with more frequent progress reporting, the task force recommended that the school change from two 9-week grading periods per semester to three 6-week grading periods. It also recommended that all students receive a progress report at the midpoint of each 6-week period. The effect of this change meant that both Stevenson staff and parents would have a report of each student's learning, in every course, every 3 weeks.

Providing Extra Time and Support for Students Who Experience Difficulty

There was great hope among the staff that these initiatives—placement by proficiency, a more proactive support system, and a comprehensive plan to assist students in making the transition to high school—would lead to success for very student. Regrettably, they did not.

It soon became evident that some students continued to flounder—notwithstanding all of the hard work of classroom teachers and despite the collective effort of the staff to create a school climate that supported learning. It also became evident that the commitment to monitor each student's learning on a more timely basis would accomplish little unless the school was prepared to respond when it discovered that a student was experiencing difficulty. Ultimately, in spite of all they had done to support students, the teachers and administrators of Stevenson could not escape the question, "What are we prepared to do when a student does not learn?" The collective response to that question became known as the Stevenson Pyramid of Interventions.

The Pyramid of Interventions

The Student Support Team

Any system of interventions for students will only be as effective as the process that is in place both to monitor student learning and to respond when students experience difficulty. Stevenson organized its Student Services Department into Student Support Teams (SSTs). The effectiveness of the school's Pyramid of Interventions continues to depend upon the work of these teams.

The SSTs are comprised of a counselor, a social worker, and the Dean of Students who share responsibility for the same group of students. The members of the team meet each week to review reports and computer printouts that offer insights into a student's academic progress, attendance, and behavior as well as anecdotal accounts regarding concern for the well-being of a student. It is the team's responsibility to initiate the appropriate assistance whenever these indicators suggest a student is experiencing difficulty.

Conferencing and Optional Tutoring

When progress reports issued at the end of the first 3 weeks of the grading period indicate students are in danger of failing, students face a cadre of adults expressing concern. The classroom teacher is asked to meet with the student, suggest strategies to improve the situation, and offer the student passes from a supervised study hall to the tutoring center. Advisors receive a copy of the progress report from every course for all of their students and meet with each student to review the reports. The advisor will counsel the student, suggest the student take advantage of additional support in the tutoring center, and assign the mentor to assist the student with homework each day. The counselor, who is also armed with a copy of the progress report, will stop in on the advisory during the week. The counselor will also meet with each student, express concern, and ask the student what steps he or she has taken to improve the situation. The parents receive a copy of the progress report and are urged to address the matter with their child. At this point, students begin to get the impression that they are being quadruple-teamed from people harassing them about their unacceptable academic performance. When confronted with this level of support (or perhaps scrutiny from the perspective of the student), most students recognize that they will not be allowed to slack off and decide to put forth sufficient effort to improve the situation—if only to ease the pressure and attention from the school personnel (and parents).

Mandatory Tutoring Program

If, despite all of this attention, students earn a grade of D or F at the end of the 6-week grading period, the SST will assign those students to mandatory tutoring. Students are no longer invited to get extra help from tutors; they are *required* to do so. Students are assigned to the tutoring center rather than supervised study hall for 2 days each week. Classroom teachers provide tutors with materials, assignment sheets, and upcoming dates for tests and projects, and tutors work with students to meet the standards established in each of their classrooms. The progress of students assigned to mandatory tutoring is monitored on a weekly basis in any course the student was not passing with a grade of C or higher. When students fail to demonstrate improvement, the SST considers moving them to the next level of intervention: Guided Study.

Guided Study Program

Most of the study halls at Stevenson have between 80 and 100 students assigned to them each period. The Guided Study Program has no more than 10 students in a given period. Whereas students in traditional study halls are required only to maintain an atmosphere conducive to study, in Guided Study hall they are required to complete their work under the direct supervision of the Guided Study teacher. Prior to assigning students to Guided Study, the SST meets with students and their parents to clarify expectations and develop a contract specifying what all parties pledge to do to help the student be successful. Both students and parents are expected to make and observe commitments regarding the changes they intend to initiate to help the student experience academic success. An attempt is made to clarify any personal or family issues that are contributing to the student's difficulty.

The goal of the Guided Study Program is to provide students with the skills, disposition, and direct supervision to ensure they complete their work and begin to experience academic success. The Guided Study teacher works with students on such study skills as using an assignment notebook, creating a schedule to ensure the timely completion and submission of homework, and developing strategies to prepare for tests. She also contacts the classroom teachers and asks to be kept informed regarding the classroom behavior, grades, pending projects, tests, and homework of each student assigned to her program. She becomes not only a liaison between students and teachers but also between parents and the school staff. She contacts the parents of all Guided Study students on a weekly basis to review the progress the student is making.

The Mentor Program

The Guided Study Program has been extremely effective in raising the achievement levels of students placed in the program, but a small percentage of students fail to respond to this support. When that occurs, the SST and the Guided Study teacher convene to determine if the student should be moved to the next step in this systematic approach to intervention: the Mentor Program. This program provides two periods of support each day in a small group setting of 10 students to one teacher and participants earn one credit toward graduation each semester. The first hour of the program operates similarly to Guided Study with the mentor teacher ensuring that students complete all homework and assignments. She insists on reviewing all of a student's work before it is turned in to the classroom teacher.

The second hour of the program is quasi-therapeutic as the mentor teacher attempts to help students and parents identify the reasons a child is choosing to fail. The teacher works in close alliance with a social worker, and one day each week is devoted to the social worker leading group processes. Students with specific problems that are interfering with academic success—substance abuse, anger management issues, grief, and so on—are also enrolled in a series of student support groups that meet each week to help students address their issues. The mentor and social worker also set aside one evening each month to meet with parents in support groups designed to help parents acquire the skills that will make them effective partners in the effort to help their students be successful in high school.

The key to both the Guided Study and Mentor programs is the ability of the teachers to develop a connection with students who have typically been alienated from school. These teachers have a special interest in working with academically at-risk students and a commitment to persevere in the face of student indifference. They monitor students closely, insist upon the completion of homework and assignments, and celebrate with students each time one of them is able to improve a grade.

The Powerful Benefits of Collective Efforts

The decision to move beyond the question, "Do we believe all kids can learn?" to address the question, "What are we prepared to do as a school when they do not learn?" has produced powerful benefits for students and staff alike at Stevenson High School. The combined D/F rate has dropped from more than 30% to less than 5%. Stevenson students excel on national assessments and consistently score among the top 1% of the schools in Illinois on each area of the comprehensive state examinations. They write more advanced placement examinations than any comprehensive high school in the world. Most significantly, every academic indicator tracked by the school has continued to improve over two decades. The school has not yet achieved its goal of "Success for Every Student," but staff members take justifiable pride in the powerful results their collective efforts have produced to date, even as they look for additional ways to reach all students.

Note: For a video representation of the material in chapters 2 and 3 (a traditional school approach to a student who is not learning versus the Stevenson Pyramid of Interventions approach), contact Solution Tree regarding the resource *Through New Eyes: Examining the Culture of Your School* at 1-800-733-6786.

Chapter 4

Overcoming Logistical Barriers
at Adlai Stevenson

"We are all faced with a series of great opportunities—brilliantly disguised as insoluble problems."

—John Gardner, 2004

"Patience and perseverance have a magical affect
before which difficulties disappear and obstacles
vanish."

—John Quincy Adams

Virtually all of the various aspects of the Pyramid of
Interventions implemented at Adlai Stevenson High
School presented logistical problems that required resolution. For example, although the advisory program seemed
to have great potential for assisting students, the questions of
who would serve as advisors and when the advisory period
would be scheduled during the school day posed formidable
problems.

The Teacher Association

The negotiated contract between the Teacher Association and the school district had always stipulated that the eight-period teacher workday would consist of teaching five periods, supervising students for one period, a duty-free lunch period, and a preparation period. The contract made no mention of assigning teachers to direct an advisory program. Furthermore, every available teacher had been assigned to one of the three traditional supervisory assignments: monitoring students in study halls, in the cafeteria, or in the hallways.

By the early 1980s the student day at Stevenson had been well established for over 15 years. Every student was assigned to six classes, a lunch period, and a study hall during the eight-period day. Where could the school find the time to provide freshmen with an advisory period? Extending the school day was not an option; to do so would violate the teacher contract.

Furthermore, students could opt out of study hall only if they enrolled in a seventh course, a choice few students elected. Study halls were held in individual teacher classrooms with approximately 25 students per study hall. Thus, providing 1,600 students with study hall meant assigning 64 teachers to that supervisory duty. The commitment of personnel to study hall left no staff available for advisory. Although the advisory program seemed like a worthwhile concept, there seemed to be no time in the day to schedule it and no teachers available to serve as advisors.

Rather than let the concept die, proponents of the advisory program began to brainstorm solutions to these problems. If upperclassmen who maintained good grades and demonstrated good behavior were no longer required to attend study hall but were given a free period instead, the number of teachers assigned to study hall could be cut in half. If study halls for the freshmen and sophomores were held in large-group venues that could accommodate 100 students rather than in classrooms limited to 25 students, the number of teachers assigned to study hall could be reduced even further. In fact, implementing these two ideas cut the number of teachers assigned to monitor study halls from 64 to 8. Since only 16 teachers were needed to serve as advisors for the entire freshman class, there were more than enough teachers available to take on the role.

The Teacher Association had several legitimate concerns about this new assignment that had to be addressed and resolved. The contract stipulated that any teacher who taught a sixth assignment would receive extra compensation, so it was agreed that advisors would not be asked to teach any content or lessons to their freshmen.

A New Concept of Supervision

The Teacher Association also pointed out that the advisory assignment would ask teachers to go far beyond their traditional supervisory responsibilities. As a study hall monitor, teachers were expected only to maintain a quiet, orderly atmosphere that was conducive to learning. Hall monitors merely checked students for passes, and cafeteria monitors simply oversaw students while they were eating to ensure they observed the rules of the school. An advisor would be expected to get to know each of his students personally, to monitor their grades and progress reports, to intervene and assist students when they were experiencing difficulty, to contact parents, and so on. The association was concerned that this new assignment represented a major extension of the traditional supervisory role.

This concern was resolved in two ways. First, it was agreed that only staff members who specifically volunteered to serve as advisors would be asked to do so. Second, the time advisors were required to devote to the assignment was dramatically reduced in comparison to other supervisory responsibilities. While study hall, cafeteria, and hallway assignments were for 50 minutes per day, 5 days each week, advisors met with their students for only 25 minutes per day, 4 days per week. With these two concessions in place, the association gave its blessing to the advisory program and scores of teachers volunteered for the assignment.

The issue of when to schedule the advisory program was resolved by reducing the freshman lunch period from 50 minutes to 25 minutes each day. This adjustment to the daily schedule had no impact on sophomores, juniors, and seniors but provided 25 minutes for freshmen to attend their advisory program.

When the idea of adding upperclassmen mentors to each advisory was proposed, it met with considerable skepticism. A mentor would be expected to give up half of his or her lunch period each day in order to hang out with and help freshmen. There seemed little likelihood of juniors and seniors volunteering to make that choice. Proponents of FMP came up with two strategies to assist in recruitment. First, specific upperclassmen would be recruited and told they had been invited to take on this new role because they were considered exemplary role models for freshmen. It was impressed upon students from the outset that serving as a mentor was an honor. Second, the One Wish Program was established to serve as an additional incentive for mentors. Students were told that those who agreed to serve as mentors would be granted one wish in their schedule for the upcoming year. For example, one student could ask for a specific teacher, another might ask for a specific free period, and another might ask for the same lunch period as his girlfriend. This program was the student's "genie in a bottle"— whatever schedule accommodation he or she requested, it was granted. These two strategies proved highly effective in recruiting students. After 3 years, the FMP program was so established as a valued part of Stevenson High School that the One Wish Program was canceled. Today, more than 500 upperclassmen apply to serve as mentors each year, more than twice as many as the school can use.

Providing Staffing

Providing staffing for the tutorial centers and the Guided Study Program also presented challenges. Once again, the tremendous reduction in the number of study halls had freed up teachers for other kinds of supervisory assignments. Teachers who preferred tutoring students to monitoring their behavior in study halls, the cafeteria, or hallways were encouraged to request tutoring as their supervision. The tutoring center also became a way of bringing beginning teachers into the school and easing them into the profession. For example, if the math department chair had been authorized to hire a full-time teacher, the chair had the option of splitting the assignment between two beginning teachers and assigning them to work in the tutoring center for the remainder of the school day. The new teacher would then teach three periods and be paid as a part-time teacher from the negotiated salary table. The teacher could then be assigned to the tutoring center three periods a day and paid at an hourly paraprofessional rate. This arrangement not only lightened the burden on first-year teachers who were typically overwhelmed at their introduction to teaching, but it also helped them acquire greater insights into the kinds of difficulties students have in their content areas.

A shift of resources away from remedial programs toward programs designed for intervention allowed for the creation of Guided Study and the Mentor Programs. The staffing levels of Stevenson's remedial and modified courses had been designed to create significantly smaller class sizes in those areas than in other courses. The elimination of remedial courses and the dramatic drop in the number of modified courses made it possible for the school to shift personnel away from remediation and into intervention.

Revising the Grading System

Some staff members were initially skeptical of the proposal to change the grading system from two 9-week periods per semester to three 6-week periods. Even more problematic for the staff was the idea of changing the school's approach to interim progress reports from twice per semester for students who were failing to a minimum of three times per semester for all students. Many complained that this shift would result in unreasonable demands on their already limited time. The teacher task force that proposed the change attempted to address this concern in several ways. First, they demonstrated that their proposal was more consistent with the frequent monitoring of student progress and strong parent partnerships that characterized high-performing schools. Second, they demonstrated that the use of appropriate technology made it possible for a teacher to send a computerized progress report to every student in a class in less time than it was taking to send written failure notices to the 10% of the students who were receiving notification under the current system. Finally, they proposed that the school pilot their recommendation for 6-week grading periods and interim progress reports for every student for 2 years. If at that time the changes had not had a positive impact on student achievement and had not clearly won the support of the staff, the school could revert to its former grading practices.

At the end of the 2-year pilot, it was evident that changes in the reporting of progress and grades had both sharply reduced the student failure rate and had been endorsed by the staff. Even critics had to acknowledge that the supporting technology had made the task manageable; however, some continued to resist the idea that they now were expected to answer the question, "How do I know if my students are learning?" every 3 weeks.

Discipline

The decisions to no longer require juniors and seniors to attend study hall and to shorten the freshman lunch period to create time for advisory led the school to re-think its approach to discipline. In the 1982 school year, Stevenson suspended 1,200 students. The most frequent cause of suspension was unauthorized absences, or "cutting" classes. Punishing students for not attending school by forbidding them to attend school was not only illogical but also ineffective. So Stevenson began to look for a new approach to student discipline that would provide incentives for students to do well rather than merely punish them when they did not.

The new approach was built on the premise "think positive, not punitive" and consisted of gradually escalating privileges for students who performed well in class and observed the rules of the school. Freshmen were given no privileges; they were under the direct supervision of a teacher the entire school day, received only 25 minutes for lunch, and were not allowed to leave campus. If, however, they were able to earn grades of C or higher in all their courses, and if they were able to avoid any serious discipline problems during their freshmen year, they earned the privilege of 50 minutes for lunch as a sophomore. If they could continue to meet the academic and behavioral expectations of the school, as juniors they would not only receive 50 minutes for lunch but also would have one free period during the day. During that period, juniors could go to the student lounge, the cafeteria, computer labs, library, open gym, guidance office, or a number of other areas on the campus. This free time carried the stipulation that students would not be in academic hallways or interfering with instruction in any way.

Seniors at Stevenson had life better than the faculty. They too received a 50-minute lunch period and one free period per day. Senior privileges, however, also included driving to school (they were the only students allowed to park on campus) and scheduling their free period at the beginning or end of the day according to their preferences. Most importantly from the senior perspective, they were allowed to leave the campus any time they were not scheduled for a class.

Once this system of privileges was in place, the primary disciplinary consequence utilized by the school became loss of privileges rather than out-of-school suspensions. A sophomore whose grades began to suffer or whose behavior was unacceptable lost the privilege of a 50-minute lunch period. A junior could lose the longer lunch and free period, and seniors could also lose driving and off-campus privileges. The only way students could earn back their privileges was to meet the standards that had earned them the privilege in the first place: good grades and good behavior for a designated period of time.

Several assumptions guided this new approach to discipline. The first was simply that students would be more inclined to meet the expectations of the school if they felt they benefited from doing so. Therefore, they should be offered incentives that they valued in recognition of meeting the academic and behavioral standards of the school.

The second assumption was that high schools made a mistake when they made no distinction in the way they dealt with 14-year-old freshmen and 18-year-old seniors. Freshmen needed intensive support and supervision to assist them in making a successful entry into high school. Seniors, however, were just months away from entering higher education or the work force where they would be expected to demonstrate self-discipline and act independently. To prepare them for that challenge, their high school experience should give them the opportunity for greater autonomy yet provide a safety net if they failed to make wise decisions.

The third assumption that drove this approach to discipline was that students should have multiple, ongoing opportunities to earn privileges. Students who failed to meet the established standards at the end of freshman year would continue to be limited to a 25-minute lunch period as a sophomore; however, they could receive the privilege of a longer lunch period if they earned good grades and demonstrated good behavior at the end of the first 6-week grading period of their sophomore year. Upperclassmen would lose their privileges for a designated period of time depending on the severity of the offense, but students always had the opportunity to regain the privileges. Most students were quickly able to see the correlation: good grades and good behavior result in privileges and increased autonomy while bad grades and bad behavior result in loss of privileges.

The final assumption behind this new approach to discipline was that parents should have the opportunity to require tighter supervision of their students than the approach provided. If a parent did not want a son or daughter to have a 50-minute lunch period, a free period, or the right to leave campus as a senior, that parent could ask the school to withhold the privilege from his or her son or daughter.

The loss-of-privilege concept proved to be much more effective in impacting student effort and behavior than the more punitive approach that preceded it. Instead of being told, "Here are our rules; obey them or we will punish you," students were told, "Here are the expectations of our school; meet them and you will receive greater freedom and autonomy each year." Students who were unaffected with a suspension were distraught over losing a privilege they had been looking forward to for months or years. Stevenson also created a program that required students to attend school on Saturday mornings as well as an in-school suspension program as alternatives to banning students from school. The net impact of these changes reduced the number of students suspended out of school as a percentage of the student body from 75% to less than 3%.

There is one final logistical barrier that Stevenson continues to face that should be noted. Stevenson High School has grown to over 4,000 students on a single campus. Contemporary conventional wisdom contends that large high schools cannot be effective in meeting the needs of their students. Stevenson calls that wisdom into question. It has reorganized into distinct houses or schools within the school, has created systems to ensure that every student has relationships with caring adults, and has taken steps to engage every student in the co-curricular program. It monitors the achievement of each of its 4,000 students every 3 weeks and responds with additional time and support whenever a student experiences difficulty.

Working Together to Find Solutions

Stevenson High School faced significant challenges, any one of which could have served as an excuse for not responding to the students who were in need: "The contract will not allow it," "The schedule will not allow it," "We don't have funding for additional staffing," "We have never done it that way before," or "We are just too big to concern ourselves with each student." The Stevenson staff chose instead to work together to find solutions to those barriers. Any school that tackles the issue of building systematic interventions for students will face the same challenge: Will we spend our energy explaining why it cannot be done in our setting or will we work together to do it?

Note: For a video representation of the material in chapters 2, 3, and 4 (a traditional school approach to a student who is not learning versus the Stevenson Pyramid of Interventions approach), contact Solution Tree regarding the resource *Through New Eyes: Examining the Culture of Your School* at 1-800-733-6786.

Chapter 5

Providing Time and Support for Kids in Middle School: Freeport Intermediate School

"High-performing middle schools establish norms, structures, and organizational arrangements to support and sustain their trajectory toward excellence. They have a sense of purpose that drives every facet of practice and decision-making."

—Schools to Watch, 2004a

"We do whatever it takes to close the gap. If it means we have to feed them, then we'll feed them. If it means we have to get them home after school, we'll do that. . . . We'll do whatever it takes."

—Clara Sale-Davis, Principal of Freeport Intermediate School, in Richardson, 2004, p. 62

The concept of the middle school is of relatively recent origin in North America. While public elementary schools can trace their roots to the 18th Century and the comprehensive high school was considered innovative in the late 19th Century, the middle school is a much more recent phenomenon.

One might assume that the absence of historical baggage might have made the middle school fertile ground for sowing the seeds of contemporary PLC concepts, and in many ways, the middle school model fits comfortably with PLC premises. For example, middle schools have typically been structured to support teachers working together rather than in isolation. The middle school has come under attack by some, however, who charge that the model is inattentive to academic achievement and unaccountable for results. These attacks have led advocates of middle schools to make frequent attempts to define and clarify their position on what the model represents. The criticism has also led several organizations to seek out middle schools that demonstrate extraordinary academic achievement. This chapter provides a brief overview of the middle school movement and tells the story of a wonderful middle school that serves as an excellent example of PLC concepts at work.

A Brief History of the Middle School Movement

In the early 1970s, almost 5,000 schools in the United States were organized into junior high schools composed of grades seven through nine, making that model the predominant organizational structure for delivery of educational programs to young teenagers. Thirty years later that structure was in place in only 689 schools. During that same time frame, the sixth- through eighth-grade middle school structure grew by over 400%—from 1,662 to 8,371 schools—and became the norm for American education.

In 1982 the National Middle School Association attempted to clarify the "essential elements of a true middle school." This list became a commonly cited standard for defining a middle school. Those essentials included:

- Educators knowledgeable about and committed to young adolescents

- A balanced curriculum based on student needs

- A range of organizational arrangements

- Varied instructional strategies

- A full exploratory program

- Comprehensive advising and counseling

- Continuous progress for students

- Evaluation procedures compatible with the nature of young adolescents

- Cooperative planning

- Positive school climate (pp. 10–15)

In 1989 the middle school movement gathered increasing momentum with the publication of *Turning Points: Preparing American Youth for the 21st Century* by the Carnegie Foundation's Council on Adolescent Development. *Turning Points* presented eight major recommendations for improving the education of young adolescents, including:

1. Create small communities for learning.

2. Teach a core academic program.

3. Ensure success for all students.

4. Empower teachers and administrators to make decisions about the experiences of middle grade students.

5. Staff middle grade schools with teachers who are expert at teaching young adolescents.

6. Improve academic performance through fostering the health and fitness of young adolescents.

7. Re-engage families in the education of young adolescents.

8. Connect schools with communities.

In 1995 and 2003 the National Middle School Association again attempted to clarify key elements of the middle school concept. According to the most recent report, middle schools are based on the developmental needs (social and academic) of young adolescents and are characterized by a culture that includes:

- Educators who are specifically prepared to work with young adolescents

- Courageous, collaborative leadership

- A shared vision that guides decisions

- An inviting, safe, and supportive environment

- High expectations for every member of the learning community

- Students and teachers engaged in active learning

- An adult advocate for every student

- School-initiated family and community partnerships (NMSA, 2003)

The report also asserts that successful middle schools provide:

- Curriculum that is relevant, challenging, integrative, and exploratory

- Multiple learning and teaching approaches that respond to student diversity

- Assessment and evaluation that promote quality learning

- Organizational structures that support meaningful relationships and learning

- School-wide efforts and policies that foster health, wellness, and safety

- Multifaceted guidance and support services (NMSA, 2003)

The impetus for the middle school movement was clearly the conviction that the unique needs of young adolescents required a unique school program. Although NMSA acknowledges academic achievement should be a "priority responsibility" for middle schools, it calls upon middle school educators to balance academic rigor with "humanness." As one of the association's position papers states:

> During the middle school years (students) face new academic demands that quite often do not coincide with their intellectual or mental development. Therefore, while intellectual development is and must continue to be the basic responsibility of the middle school, the education and nurture of young adolescents has to be an integrated venture that provides a balance between academic rigor and humanness. The physical, social, emotional, and intellectual aspects of young adolescents are inexorably woven together in the fabric of their lives. (2004, p. 1)

The authors of *Turning Points 2000* (Jackson & Davis, 2000) contend that "the middle school movement reflects the grassroots genius of American educators," but the movement has not been without its critics. One of the most consistent criticisms of the concept is the charge that middle schools are inattentive to academic rigor and ineffective in helping students achieve high standards. The NMSA assertion that the "intellectual and mental development" of many adolescents leaves them unprepared to meet new academic challenges has been cited as evidence of the low expectations for learning that allegedly permeate middle schools.

One of the most aggressive attacks upon middle schools came from Cheri Pierson Yecke, the commissioner of Education of Minnesota, who charged that middle schools have waged a war against academic excellence and have fostered mediocrity. Using the strident rhetoric reminiscent of *A Nation at Risk,* Yecke (2003) asserted that "radical middle school activists view the public schools as their personal vehicle for engineering an egalitarian society, in complete disregard for what the American public desires" (p. 13). She charged that NMSA has encouraged middle schools to reduce the rigor of the entire middle school curriculum, a strategy that has been particularly harmful to gifted children who have been systematically reduced to underachievers.

Although Yecke may be the most extreme in her attack against the middle school concept, she is not alone in questioning its effectiveness. Richard Mills, state education commissioner of New York expressed concern about the lack of focus of middle schools after 5 years of testing data demonstrated widespread failure across the state. The city of New

York has been so discouraged by the performance of its middle schools that it has developed a plan to eliminate the structure and convert its schools to either kindergarten through eighth grade or sixth through twelfth grade (Herszenhorn, 2004).

Is it possible for middle schools to promote both high levels of learning for all students and a humane school environment sensitive to the unique needs of young adolescents? Several organizations were determined to find out. The National Forum to Accelerate Middle-Grades Reform was developed in 1997 "out of a sense of urgency that middle-grades school improvement had stalled, amid a flurry of descending test scores, increasing reports of school violence, and heated debates about the nature and purpose of middle-grades education" (2004). Convinced that schools did not have to "choose between equity and excellence," this organization envisioned middle schools where all students were achieving at significantly higher levels. The National Forum created 34 criteria to describe high-performing middle schools, and in 2000 set out to find schools that met the criteria. Four schools were identified as national models.

The National Association of Secondary School Principals was also interested in finding exemplary middle schools and asked Dr. Jerry Valentine, director of the Middle Level Leadership Center, to help identify those schools. Valentine invited state departments of education and a variety of national organizations to identify exemplary middle school programs and received 275 nominations representing all 50 states. Nominated schools were invited to complete an extensive application, and an independent panel then narrowed the field to 100 schools on the basis of their ability to document meeting student needs and implementing the recommendations presented in *Turning Points 2000.* These remaining schools were subjected to another round of data collection that included surveys from teachers, students, and parents. Based on that information, six schools were selected for site visits in the spring of 2002, and ultimately those six were declared "Highly Effective Middle Schools." Each of the six was lauded for "commitment to individual student success," "a culture of collaboration," and "continuous and collective learning among teachers" (Valentine, 2004)—key concepts of the PLC model.

An Exemplary Middle School: Freeport Intermediate

The only middle school selected as a national model by both the National Forum and the NASSP study was Freeport Intermediate School, one of the schools in the Brazosport Independent School District. Located approximately 50 miles south of Houston, Freeport offers grades seven and eight to 589 students, 70% of whom are eligible for free or reduced priced lunches.

Freeport's efforts have been guided by the Eight Step Improvement Process (Richardson, 2004), a district initiative to implement Total Quality Management principles in all Brazosport schools. Those steps include:

Step 1: Disaggregate data, including test results.

Step 2: Develop an instructional calendar.

Step 3: Deliver the instructional focus, based on the calendar.

Step 4: Assess student mastery of the standard taught.

Step 5:   Provide additional instruction for students who did not master the assessment.

Step 6:   Provide enrichment for students who did master the assessment.

Step 7:   Provide ongoing maintenance of standards taught.

Step 8:   Monitor the process.

When the staff of Freeport Intermediate began this process by disaggregating data, the results were not pretty. High failure rates were strongly correlated with discipline referrals and high absenteeism. Freeport students' scores on the statewide assessment were among the worst in Texas, and the state had designated Freeport as a "low performing" school. But according to Freeport principal Clara Sale-Davis, this analysis of the evidence of student achievement helped to create a sense of urgency that was critical in the transformation of the school. As staff members honestly confronted the data on student achievement, they built shared knowledge on the current reality of their school, recognized the need for change, and began to work together to improve results rather than excuse them.

Sale-Davis knew that building a collaborative culture was critical to the success of the school's improvement initiative. The schedule that was in place when she became principal of Freeport provided ample time for teachers to work together during the school day. An alternating A/B block schedule gave teachers 90 minutes to work with their interdisciplinary team one day and their subject area team the next. But Freeport's experience demonstrated that while providing a staff with time to work together is a necessary condition for a collaborative culture, it is not sufficient. Sale-Davis faced the more formidable challenge of creating a systematic process to ensure that teams would use their collaborative time in ways that would impact student achievement.

Sale-Davis met that challenge by providing her teachers with the structures, parameters, and priorities essential to results-oriented teams. She asked teachers on every team to study their state standards, clarify essential outcomes for students, and develop an instructional calendar to ensure all students would have access to a core curriculum that could be addressed in the allotted time. In other words, each team clarified exactly what each student was to learn.

The teams then turned their attention to the second critical question of a learning community—How will we know if students are learning?—and began to develop common assessments to monitor the proficiency of each student. At the conclusion of each instructional focus (or approximately once each week), teacher teams administer brief common assessments to all students in the same grade level. Each quarter the teams administer a common cumulative exam. Each spring the teams develop and administer practice tests for the state exam. Each year the teams carefully analyze the results of the state test, and each teacher can see how his or her students performed on every skill and on every item of the test. The teachers share their results from all of these assessments with their colleagues and quickly learn when a teammate has been particularly effective in teaching a particular skill. Teams consciously look for successful practice and then attempt to replicate it throughout the team. The ongoing analysis also helps teams identify areas of the curriculum that need more attention.

But, once again, monitoring student achievement does little to promote learning unless the school is prepared to give students who are experiencing difficulty additional time and support. So Freeport restructured its daily schedule to ensure students would have the time to master the core curriculum. Its block schedule provides instructional periods of 90 minutes. Students attend language arts and mathematics classes each day and attend social studies, science, and elective classes every other day. The daily schedule ensures that students have extra time to master literacy and numeracy.

Team Time

Furthermore, at the end of each school day, Freeport students are assigned to 1 hour of "team time." This hour is specifically designed for flexible grouping. Students who have not mastered a skill are assigned to one teacher for additional support while those who have demonstrated proficiency are assigned to other teachers for enrichment. Because the teams are checking for student understanding every week at the conclusion of each instructional focus, the makeup of the groups at team time remains fluid. As Sale-Davis explains, "We check for understanding in a variety of ways using lots of little, timely assessments. We found that if you continually assess, you can nip problems in the bud as soon as the student has trouble with a concept."

Spiraling Instruction

One problem with short-term assessments is that students can become conditioned to learn in the short term, only preparing enough to meet the standard for a weekly assessment but retaining little beyond the weekend. Freeport teachers counteract that tendency by spiraling their instruction to ensure that students maintain the skills they have learned. The quarterly comprehensive assessments are also used to monitor student retention of essential knowledge and skills. Once again, students are re-grouped during their team period based on their proficiency on these quarterly assessments. Teachers who are responsibile for tutoring students who are not yet proficient are chosen because of their expertise and passion. The teams know which member is most skillful in teaching a particular concept and call upon that teacher to work with students who are most in need while other teachers on the team extend learning for students through enrichment activities.

Benchmark Testing

Students can be re-grouped during their team time yet again in early March when they take a benchmark test in preparation for their state test. If the results indicate a student still has not acquired the knowledge and skills to be proficient on the upcoming state test, the school provides even more time and support for that student. For the 2 months prior to the state test, Freeport runs an extended day program that meets for 1 hour before and after school 3 days per week. Although attendance in the program is by invitation, the school impresses upon parents (through letters, phone calls, and even home visits if necessary) that any student who is not proficient should attend. The school provides snacks for students to boost their energy level and provides buses for students who face transportation issues. As a result of this emphasis and support, the school has been remarkably successful in having parents and students understand that the program is essential preparation for success. Last year, 77 of the 80 students recommended for the extended day participated in the program.

This program has been funded by shifting dollars from the summer school remedial program for students who had failed the state test to this powerful intervention to prevent the failure. The impact is evident. Remedial summer school enrollment has dropped by 80%.

From Low Expectations to Exemplary Performance

In an article from the *Houston Chronicle,* Freeport staff members describe their school as a place "with a story to tell" (Schools to Watch, 2004b), and they are absolutely right. It is the story of a school that transformed itself from a tradition of low expectations to a school that has been designated as an "exemplary" school of Texas—a school in which over 90% of its students meet state standards with no gaps in achievement based on race, ethnicity, or socioeconomic status. It is a story of a school with many students coming from poverty-stricken homes that has received the United States Department of Education's Blue Ribbon Award. It is the story of a school that has received national recognition as a model of effectiveness because it provides compelling evidence that the middle school concept and high levels of learning for all students are not mutually exclusive.

Chapter 6

A School-Wide System of Time and Support for Elementary Students: Boones Mill Elementary School

"If adults don't learn, then students won't learn either. No matter how good school goals are, they cannot be met if the school isn't organized to accomplish them. The school operates as a learning community that uses its own experience and knowledge, and that of others, to improve the performance of students and teachers alike. . . . A culture of shared responsibility is established, and everybody learns from one another.

—NAESP, 2002, p. 5

"I'm not just a teacher at Boones Mill: I'm also a parent. It is very reassuring to know that if my children experience difficulty, it won't fall to a single teacher to solve the problem. At Boones Mill an entire team of adults will rally around any child who needs extra support to be successful."

—Lisa Doss, Third Grade Teacher,
Boones Mill Elementary School

Any school hoping to become a Professional Learning community, regardless of the grade levels served, must decide how to respond as a school when it becomes evident that some students are struggling to learn essential skills and concepts. The details of the school-wide system designed to provide students with extra time and support during the school day will vary from level to level, but the critical question of "How do we respond when kids don't learn?" is just as necessary and powerful at the elementary school level as it is at the middle school and high school levels.

Boones Mill Elementary School in Franklin County, Virginia, could be considered the antithesis of Stevenson High School in many ways, including size, resources, and the students and community it serves. Boones Mill draws its 400 K–5 students from a rural area of south-central Virginia that has been hit hard by the loss of jobs in the textile and furniture manufacturing industries. The per-pupil expenditure of the Franklin County school division ranks in the bottom 10% of the Commonwealth of Virginia, yet its students face the same rigorous testing challenges as schools in much more affluent areas of the state.

Virginia offers a prototypical model of a state that has embraced high stakes testing. In 1995, the Virginia Department of Education issued the revised K–12 Standards of Learning (SOLs) to all schools throughout the commonwealth, standards that identified rigorous student outcomes by grade level in the areas of English (reading, writing, listening, speaking, research), mathematics, science, social studies, and technology. State assessments were developed for certain grade levels and courses, and schools were informed that if at least 70% of their students did not meet the minimum proficiency score on the assessments within a few years, the school would receive sanctions up to and including loss of state accreditation. The first time the tests were administered, only 2% of the schools across the Commonwealth met the 70% target.

Few could have predicted that Boones Mill, this small school in rural Virginia with very few resources, would become one of the most successful in the Commonwealth in helping students meet the new standards. This achievement is even more dramatic in light of the fact that the school includes all of its students in testing rather than utilizing the option of excluding some special needs students. Furthermore, every indicator that the school uses to monitor student learning—at the building, district, state, and national levels—has been on a steady climb upward since implementing the PLC model of continuous school improvement.

A Critical First Step: Building Shared Knowledge of the Current Reality

Like most schools, Boones Mill was staffed with hard-working, dedicated educators who sincerely wanted to help all students achieve at high levels. Ultimately, the staff concluded that the best hope of achieving that goal was to embrace the concepts of a PLC. Eventually the entire staff grappled with the third critical question: How will we respond, as a school, when it becomes evident that some students are not learning what is being taught despite our best efforts in the classroom?

The staff began their exploration of this question by building shared knowledge about the current reality in their school as they generated a comprehensive list of practices already in place to address the needs of struggling learners. Like other elementary schools in the district, Boones Mill offered a 4-week summer school program for "recommended" students in grades K–5, but participation was not required. Other options for additional time and support included retention at that grade level, promotion to the next grade level with the hope that the difficulty was simply "developmental," or referral for special education testing and services.

Outside of those limited options, the issue of whether or how to intervene for struggling students was left to the discretion of each individual teacher. Traditionally, a few teachers offered tutorial sessions before and/or after school. Student attendance at the sessions, however, was by invitation and the students who were most in need of extra support were typically the least likely to stay to receive it. Family transportation issues, conflicts with co-curricular activities, or lack of parental insistence on their participation allowed students to "opt out."

Many teachers were not in a position to offer extra time and support beyond the student day because of competing professional, personal, and family obligations. Several of those teachers attempted to create opportunities for interventions during the school day; however, they faced the question of "when and how?" Some grade-level teams decided to use student recess time for intervention with certain teachers assigned to supervise the students in "free play" while one teacher volunteered to work with struggling learners. This strategy, however well intentioned, did not please some parents and most students. Struggling learners were often denied a much-needed break and ultimately came to view the additional help as punishment.

A few teachers used their own duty-free lunch periods to provide a "working lunch" for students who needed more time, but again the students were not required to attend. Most students, especially those in the upper elementary grades, chose to eat lunch with their peers in the cafeteria rather than work with their teachers.

As state accountability sanctions grew closer, "specials classes" (such as art, music, physical education, computers, library skills, and guidance) were suspended and the specials teachers were required to tutor students in the core curriculum for the grade levels facing state assessments. Although this strategy for improving results on the state assessments was clearly misaligned with the school's mission to promote growth in each area of development, it seemed justified because desperate times called for desperate measures.

Referring students for special education services also became an attractive option for providing additional time and support. A student with an Individual Educational Plan (IEP) was guaranteed extra academic assistance and was typically exempted from some of the consequences faced by regular education students when they failed to meet the proficiency standards of district or state testing: summer school, loss of elective classes in middle school, after-school remediation the following school year, Saturday school, and so on.

This collective study of and dialogue about the current reality of the school helped the staff come to consensus on the following conclusions:

- The school had no human resources other than teachers to provide additional time and support for struggling learners.

- Individual teachers responded to students who were not learning in very different ways.

- The only students getting extra support from adults beyond the classroom teacher during the school day were those eligible for special education services and a few primary grade students who received assistance in phonemic awareness skills from a part-time paraprofessional tutor.

- Even though the school had several reliable volunteers, a solid, systematic process of interventions could not be dependent on volunteers.

- An after-school program of tutorial support that depend on the willingness and/or ability of students to attend was insufficient to ensure that all students who experienced difficulty would receive extra time and support for learning.

- An honest assessment of the collective response of the school to students who were not learning could only lead to the conclusion that the response was limited, untimely, and random rather than systematic.

As the staff confronted this reality, they agreed purposeful change was imperative if the school was to achieve the goal of high levels of learning for all students. That conclusion resulted in their willingness to initiate the team learning process.

The Team Learning Process

The staff agreed that in order for a comprehensive system of student support to be effective, it was incumbent upon every team to identify each student who needed assistance on a timely basis, to use consistent standards and processes in identifying those students, and to pinpoint the specific skill each student was having difficulty in mastering. Teaching teams of all the teachers of a grade level and the special education teacher who served that grade level were able to meet these challenges by engaging in a 5-step team learning process.

Step One: Identify the 16 to 20 most essential outcomes (knowledge and skills) that all students MUST learn in each content area at each grade level this school year.

Each team began the process of clarifying essential outcomes by collectively studying local, state, and national resources such as state standards; district curriculum guides; national standards (when applicable); district reading and writing rubrics; the district's standards-based report card; checklists of skills; district, state, and national summative assessments, and the data generated from those assessments; "wish lists" of critical skills identified by teachers at the next grade level; textbooks; and teacher-made units of instruction from previous years.

As team members built shared knowledge regarding the content of these resources, developed common understandings, and clarified misconceptions or ambiguity regarding the meaning of certain standards, they were asked to produce a list of the 16 to 20 *most essential outcomes* for that grade level in each subject area and to align those outcomes with stated standards and district curriculum guides.

The teams began the process by focusing on mathematics, which seemed less susceptible to a variety of interpretations than other subject areas. Once the outcomes for math were identified, each team turned its attention to the essential outcomes for language arts. By the end of the semester, each team had agreed on the essential outcomes for these two critical areas of the curriculum.

Teams then began dialogue regarding the best way to sequence the content of the curriculum to ensure all students achieved the essential outcomes. Common pacing guides for each grade level were developed as a result of this dialogue. Each team worked with the teams above and below its grade level to ensure vertical articulation and to identify any gaps or overlaps in the curriculum. The lists of outcomes and common pacing guides were also shared with support service staff, parents, and community volunteers who worked with students so that all those involved in helping students could operate from the same knowledge base. The curriculum of the school became more connected and more public than ever before.

Step Two: Develop at least four formative common assessments designed to assist each team in answering the question, "How will we know when each child has learned the essential outcomes?"

Once again teams built shared knowledge by studying best practice in assessment in an attempt to determine the most equitable, valid, and authentic ways to monitor each student's mastery of essential skills and concepts. All teams became students of the district, state, and national assessments their students would take and shared examples of the assessments that individual members of the team had created over the years.

As a result of this joint study, each team created a variety of common assessments that were to be administered to all the students in the grade level following an initial period of instruction that corresponded to the team pacing guide. Some of the common assessments were traditional multiple choice, true/false, fill-in-the-blank, or short-answer tests, but others were performance-based using portfolios, writing prompts, projects, independent reading inventories, and oral presentations with supporting team-made rubrics or checklists.

In order to draw valid conclusions regarding student achievement when performance-based assessments were used, teams had to address two significant challenges. First, all members of the team had to agree on the criteria by which they would judge the quality of student work. All teachers had to be so clear on the team's definitions of what excellent, above average, good, below average, and poor student work looked like on their common assessment that they could clearly describe that criteria to each other, their students, and parents. Second, all members of that same team had to apply those criteria consistently. In other words, they had to establish inter-rater reliability.

In order to address those challenges, team members practiced applying their agreed-upon criteria to random, anonymous samples of student work. As long as the variation in scoring was no more than one point on a five-point scale, the team felt they were demonstrating inter-rater reliability. If, however, any two members of the same team varied more than one point, the team stopped, discussed the ratings and the criteria they had established, and worked until they could agree on the application of the criteria.

Teams found they also needed consistency in the administration of assessments. For example, when using oral assessments, the members of the team had to agree on guidelines for administration—the setting, allowable "wait time" before the student would be expected to respond, whether prompting was appropriate, and so on. Of course, an exception to this consistent administration of assessments was made for any special education student whose IEP identified specific accommodations that were to be extended to the student.

Step Three: Set a target score all students must achieve to demonstrate proficiency in each skill on each common assessment.

As each common assessment was developed, the team set a benchmark score that each student would be required to attain to demonstrate proficiency. The score was intended to be fair, yet challenging. For example, some targets were established at 80% out of 100 possible points while others required a minimum score of three on a five-point rubric. The proficiency target was to remain the same for all students—even those struggling to learn the skills and concepts being taught. Teams were to operate with the assumption that with appropriate levels of time and support, *every* student could demonstrate proficiency on the essential outcomes.

Step Four: Administer the common assessments and analyze results.

Each team agreed to administer its common assessment according to the timetable established in the team pacing guide. Group assessments were typically administered at the same time and on the same day in order to promote consistent testing conditions. Individual assessments, such as independent reading inventories, were completed during an agreed-upon window of time established by the team.

After the assessments were administered to all students in each grade level, individual teachers submitted their class scores to the principal who compiled grade-level data that were promptly forwarded to the team for analysis. To relieve initial teacher anxiety and to emphasize that the assessments were intended to be formative rather than summative (assessment *for* learning rather than assessment *of* learning), the principal promised never to share a teacher's individual classroom results with anyone other than the teacher and never to use the results in a teacher's evaluation. No teacher would be able to rank his or her performance with that of a colleague. No teacher would be cited for having the worst results on the assessments or lauded for having the best. The team, however, was expected to work together to analyze the results for all students and to identify areas of concern.

Step Five: Celebrate strengths and identify and implement improvement strategies.

The data from the common assessments made it possible for all teams to identify program strengths—skills and concepts in which all or almost all students achieved the team's target. Not only did the teams "pat themselves on the back" for a job well done (as they should!), but they were also able to identify and recognize individual students for high achievement or notable improvement. At the same time, however, each team also identified at least one area of their program that could be improved. Furthermore, individual teachers were able to identify problem areas in their teaching and then call upon teammates for help in addressing those areas. This process enhanced the effectiveness of both the team and its individual members. As Mike Schmoker (2003) writes, "instructional improvement depends on such simple, data-driven formats—teams identifying and addressing areas of difficulty and then developing, critiquing, testing, and upgrading efforts in light of ongoing results" (p. 24).

Most importantly, this team learning process identified any student who had not achieved the target proficiency score on each skill or concept being assessed. That information was of little use, however, unless the school was able to develop an effective system of providing those students with additional time and support for learning. Creating procedures for identifying students who needed help was a critical step, but the crucial question remained: Now that we know which students have not achieved the intended standards, how do we intend to respond?

Shifting Resources to Provide Time and Support for Students

At that point, the staff began to brainstorm possibilities for providing students with additional time and support for learning during the school day. As a result of those discussions, the principal proposed and the faculty enthusiastically endorsed shifting some site-based funds designated for the purchase of instructional materials to support the hiring of a part-time "floating tutor" to assist each grade-level team when a student was not learning. That decision by the staff led to a significant logistical challenge: When could the tutor have access to students who needed additional time and support? The principal gave teams latitude in answering that question, provided the solution met the following parameters:

1. Each grade-level team had to make its students accessible to the tutor for a minimum of 30 minutes per day.

2. The tutorial time identified had to be consistent and constant among all classrooms in the grade level. By making all the students of a grade level available at the same time, the tutor could work with six grade-level units rather than 20 independent classrooms.

3. The designated time could not conflict with any direct instructional blocks (such as language arts, math, science, social studies, and specials classes).

4. The tutorial time could not interfere with the student's recess or other fun activities. The extra time and support should not be presented or perceived as punishment.

The person hired to fill the part-time tutor position was a district-certified substitute teacher who had worked extensively at Boones Mill, had proven to be effective in classrooms at all grade levels, and related well with students, staff, and the parent community. She worked from a faculty-created job description that was designed to provide maximum flexibility and to accommodate the flow of different students in and out of services since, typically, the same students did not require tutorial services in all essential skills. Under the team's direction, the tutor could:

- Provide supplementary instruction or intervention for individuals or small groups of no more than eight students on specific activities designed by the grade-level team.

- Review, model, and practice test-taking skills and strategies with students, helping them to feel more confident in responding to a variety of assessment tasks and instruments.

- Supervise classroom activities during the grade-level's designated tutorial time to allow the certified teachers to work with identified students on essential skills and concepts.

Once each team had designated a daily time for intervention and enrichment activities, the school's volunteer program became much more effective in terms of providing support for learning. A school-based volunteer committee, co-led by parents and teachers, worked together to solicit and assign volunteers throughout the school according to requests from individual classrooms and teams. Over time, many parents, grandparents, business partners, senior citizens, college students, and high-school interns considering education as a career option were scheduled into the grade-level tutorial times to assist students and provide more one-on-one support.

Each grade-level team decided how to group their students during daily tutorial time so all students, not just the students needing intervention, could benefit. This protected block of time allowed teams to differentiate instruction and to meet the needs of all learners in unprecedented ways. For example, the kindergarten and first-grade teams created grade-level learning centers by moving learning centers from their individual classrooms to a common area outside their classrooms. Teachers then contributed their best activities from their individual classrooms to each center and aligned those activities with the team pacing guides for each content area. Second- through fifth-grade teams elected to engage students who had mastered the essential skills in individual and group activities including computer-based learning and exploration, silent sustained reading, Junior Great Books reading circles, and teacher read-alouds while their classmates received tutoring. In these grade levels, the tutor typically supervised the classroom activity while one of the teachers on the team provided the tutoring.

Within 2 months, the floating tutorial program was so successful that the faculty decided to suspend the traditional voluntary after-school remediation program. The staff was convinced that the floating tutorial program was so superior that it sought and received the district's permission to use the state remediation money that had funded the after-school program to hire a second floating tutor to assist students during the school day.

By the beginning of second semester, Boones Mill had a team of two floating tutors working in tandem each day according to the following schedule:

8:20–8:50	Fifth Grade
8:50–9:20	Fourth Grade
9:30–10:30	First-Grade Centers
10:30–11:30	Kindergarten Centers
11:35–12:15	Third Grade
12:20–12:50	Duty-Free Lunch
1:00–1:30	Second Grade
1:30–2:00	Additional Time K–5 (By Request)
2:00–2:30	Fifth Grade
2:30–2:50	Remediation Record Keeping/ Team Communication

The floating tutorial services served as the foundation for the Boones Mill program for providing students who had not mastered essential outcomes with additional time and support. It ensured that every student was now guaranteed to receive timely, directive, systematic intervention during the school day whenever that student struggled with initial learning. Even with that system in place, the dedicated staff continued to create other strategies to assist students.

Grade-Level Parent Workshops

The staff concluded that parents could become a powerful source to support learning for their children *if* they were armed with the right tools and guidelines. Therefore, within the first 4 weeks of each new semester, grade-level teams conducted workshops for all parents who had students in their grade level. These workshops were advertised in advance to parents both through school and grade-level publications and were coordinated on the school's calendar so that no other school event conflicted with any workshop.

The grade-level parent workshops were structured to provide parents with a program overview: key concepts of the curriculum, instructional strategies, purpose and format of assessments, and special events their students would experience during the coming months. Most importantly, the teams provided parents with practice/tutorial packets aligned with the essential outcomes in language arts and math. Teachers then guided parents through the content of the packets so parents could use the materials at home with their children to reinforce essential skills. Parents who attended the workshops left with a good understanding of the expectations the team had for students at that grade level. They also understood that their child was part of a clearly defined program of studies that was not solely dependent on the classroom to which he or she had been assigned, but was instead guided by the experience and expertise of all members of the collaborative team.

Parents who were unable to attend the workshops were sent the packet of materials with a cover letter from the team explaining the contents. A few days later the homeroom teacher contacted those parents to discuss the packet and answer any questions they might have.

Peer Tutoring/Buddy Programs

Another successful layer of time and support for students in all grades was the focused attention on peer tutoring and "Buddy" systems. Teams found there were frequent opportunities for peer tutoring within individual classrooms and between classes in any particular grade. Because all classes at each grade had a common schedule—that is designated times for instruction in each content area, specials instruction, lunch, recess, planning, and so on—teachers could easily structure flexible groups based on skills, partnerships, cooperative learning teams, and study groups without disrupting routine.

In addition to peer tutoring within grade levels, the faculty also established inter-grade partnerships, or buddy programs, where older students served as tutors, reading buddies, mentors, and role models for the younger students. For example, during the first year of the PLC, the principal structured a K–5 buddy program that not only provided time for the students at these two grade levels to come together and learn from each other every week, but also gave the kindergarten and fifth grade teaching teams time to collaborate.

Save One Student Program

Another support program created by the Boones Mill staff was the Save One Student, or SOS, program, which called upon each adult in the building to take a personal interest in a student who was at risk academically and to assist that student by providing the gifts of time and support. The SOS students were identified by their classroom teachers as children who would benefit from regular contact with another friendly, caring adult at school because, for whatever reason, the students lacked an academic support system at home.

The commitment to become an SOS adult required staff members to make two or three contacts per week with his or her assigned student at times that were mutually convenient for the student and the SOS adult. The contacts were never made during direct instruction times but usually occurred when the sponsoring adult and SOS student had a common connection in their schedules. A teacher task force wrote a description of the program and established guidelines for implementation. All 42 of the adults who worked at Boones Mill volunteered for the SOS program.

Connecting Special and Regular Education

Prior to implementing the PLC model of school improvement, Boones Mill used one of its two special education teachers to assist all students with learning disabilities assigned to mainstream classes. The resource teacher typically used a "pull-out" program to provide services to all students in kindergarten through fifth grade. This presented a tremendous scheduling challenge for the single resource teacher as she struggled to help each identified student attain IEP goals and objectives in language arts and math by taking them out of 18 different classrooms, each with its own daily schedule, curriculum pacing guides, instructional strategies, and resources. This arrangement also required regular classroom teachers to keep track of make-up assignments for students pulled away from their instruction to receive special education support. Students with the greatest academic needs were either completely missing essential instruction and assignments in one content area in order to receive services in another or were being held accountable for completing assignments at home, during recess, or during specials classes with little or no direct instruction in the relevant skills and concepts.

The second special education teacher managed a K–5 "self-contained" special education classroom. The students assigned to this classroom tended to have more profound special education needs—severe developmental delays, behavioral or emotional disabilities, and medical or physical handicaps. Traditionally, these students were kept separate from their regular education peers for most or all of the day. The variety of learning levels and needs in this classroom, combined with the fact that there was only one teacher and a teacher assistant assigned to these students, meant the primary focus of the program was often managing behavior rather than teaching and learning. There were few opportunities for either the students or adults in these separate programs to interact with their regular education counterparts.

As the staff began to work together on implementing PLC concepts, the walls that separated special and regular education programs began to crumble. The special education program was redesigned to better meet the needs of both students and adults. The two special education teachers were reassigned to curriculum level teams—one teacher to the primary teams and the other to upper elementary. Both teachers worked with their grade-level colleagues to clarify the essential outcomes for each grade level, write common assessments, establish the target score, plan and deliver instruction in the essential skills, administer the common assessment to their students according to the accommodations in the IEPs, analyze the results, and identify improvement strategies. Classroom teachers helped their special education colleagues develop greater clarity regarding essential outcomes and the standards students were expected to achieve. The special education teachers advised their teammates regarding effective instructional strategies, supplementary materials, and alternative assessments for special education students. This new sense of shared responsibility for students between regular and special education teachers helped special education students experience a much more connected curriculum and achieve higher levels of learning than ever before.

Another shift that occurred in the school was its use of the Child Study Team, which began to serve as a clearinghouse for intervention strategies to help students find success in the regular education program.

Extended Coordination Among Classroom Teachers and Support Services Staff

Once the staff completed the team learning process described earlier in this chapter, each grade-level team faced the challenge of creating effective two-way systems of communication with all the adults who served their children, including the other teams, specialist teachers, tutors, and support staff. Some of the communications regarding student learning that flowed between and among teachers and support services staff are listed below.

- **Weekly Feedback Sheets** from team meetings were distributed to the principal and ad hoc team members to keep them informed of the team's current focus, questions, and concerns.

- **Weekly/Bi-Weekly Grade-Level Newsletters** to parents were also given to the principal and support services staff so that everyone was informed of essential skills, student celebrations, calendar events, and so on.

- **Monthly Vertical Team Meetings** were scheduled during student assemblies so each team could address a skill or topic with the grade level below and the grade level above it. All six teams would meet frequently to review how a concept was developed from kindergarten through fifth grade.

- **Monthly Faculty Meetings** were established with protected time at each meeting for teams to share what they were learning with the entire staff.

- **Monthly "Scoop Sheets"** were sent from each team to all specialists and support staff listing specific content and skills to be instructed at that grade level in the coming month. This helped specialists reinforce key grade-level outcomes in their program.

- **Forty-Five Minutes of Contract Time** at the end of each school day was protected from disruption to afford opportunities for classroom teachers, specialists, and support staff to engage in dialogue or schedule meetings as needed to discuss curriculum and student learning needs.

The ongoing dialogue throughout the school and coordination within and among teams enabled the entire staff to make meaningful and timely curriculum connections for students. The specials teachers were able to connect their area of expertise and passion with classroom instruction at the different grade levels because of the frequent communication flowing to and from grade-level teams. The full-time specialists assigned to Boones Mill also elected to join one grade-level team in completing a year-long action research project that culminated in curriculum and assessment products tied to the team's SMART goal—a goal that was specific, strategic, measurable, attainable, results-oriented, and time-bound (Conzemius & O'Neill, 2002).

For example, the librarian joined the second-grade team as they worked throughout the year to create multiple trade-book units of instruction complete with teacher guides, student lessons and activities, and assessment tools to enrich the reading program in second grade. The guidance counselor joined the fifth grade team in its effort to improve the social skills, study habits, and test-taking strategies of fifth graders and to assist those students (and their parents) in a smoother transition to the middle school. The music teacher wrote and produced annual musicals related to the social studies content of certain grade levels. Specialists took pride in the contributions they made to each grade-level team.

The open communication and synchronization of schedules and services benefited the staff in other ways as well. Each grade level had the benefit of an intervention team—floating tutors, special education teachers and/or teacher assistants, the part-time state-funded phonemic awareness tutor, the part-time gifted and talented resource teacher, volunteers, and mentors— to assist them in differentiating instruction to better meet the needs of all learners in a timely, systematic, and directive way. Furthermore, the coordination of services among and between grade-level teams provided each classroom teacher with large blocks of protected instructional time and few interruptions to individual classrooms throughout the day.

Hand-in-Hand, We All Learn

This intensive focus on the learning of each student, the collaborative and coordinated effort among staff members, and the systematic school-wide plan for intervention have made Boones Mill a great place for students and staff. Every staff member has the benefit of a collaborative team—colleagues to turn to and talk to when looking for better ways to meet student needs. Every student knows that the school will respond promptly with additional time and support if he or she experiences difficulty in learning. Every parent knows there will be a coordinated effort among the members of the team to provide students with a high-quality program and that a system is in place to assist their children when they need additional support.

The Boones School Motto, "Hand-in-Hand, We All Learn," captures the very essence of the PLC concept. More importantly, at Boones Mill the motto represents not merely words on school documents, but a powerful commitment to meeting the needs of students and adults that is carried out every day.

The remarkable success of Boones Mill has captured national attention. As this book goes to press, Boones Mill is one of seven schools in Virginia to be nominated for the United States Department of Education's new "No Child Left Behind Blue Ribbon Award." *The Video Journal* (2001, 2003) has featured Boones Mill in two different programs on high-performing elementary schools. Its description of this wonderful school could serve as a standard for which all schools can strive: "Boones Mill is a happy place for everyone, because the needs of everyone are fulfilled."

Chapter 7

A School-Wide System of Time and Support for Elementary Students: Los Peñasquitos Elementary School

"High expectations for success will be judged not only by the initial staff beliefs and behaviors, but also by the organization's response when some students do not learn."

—Larry Lezotte, 1991a, p. 2

"In our Los Pen pledge the staff promises, among other things, to do whatever it takes—go the extra mile—to ensure that every student achieves or exceeds grade-level academic expectations. This pledge makes up the heart and soul of what we are all about at Los Pen. It represents far more than just words; it is the fuel that energizes us as a team of professionals with a heart for student learning."

—Damen Lopez, Principal, Los Peñasquitos Elementary School

Los Peñasquitos Elementary School, located in Rancho Peñasquitos near San Diego, California, is a continent away from Boones Mill Elementary School geographically and a world away from Boones Mill in terms of the students it serves. While Boones Mill draws its students from rural Virginia, Los Pen's 748 students live in a mix of apartment buildings, low-income housing, and middle-class homes that surround the school. While Boones Mill has some ethnic and socioeconomic diversity in its student population, Los Pen's students are very diverse. They come from homes of abject poverty as well as considerable affluence. They represent dozens of nationalities and speak 28 languages. What the schools do have in common, however, are teachers who are committed to the success of *all* of their children.

The Los Pen staff began its PLC journey by clarifying and agreeing upon the mission, vision, commitments, and goals for their school—an agreement that came to be known as the "Los Pen School Pledge." The mission statement endorsed by the staff went beyond the pledge of "learning for all" to make the following bold, unequivocal assertion:

> "Everyone involved at Los Peñasquitos Elementary believes that the academic potential of each student is tremendous. We refuse to accept difficult challenges that confront some students as excuses for poor learning. We know that one of the greatest predictors of life success is educational success. Therefore, we are committed to creating a school that knows no limits to the academic success of each student."

The teachers then demonstrated that this proclamation was not merely politically correct rhetoric by pledging to:

- Accept no limits on the learning potential of any child.

- Meet the individual learning needs of each child.

- Create serious classroom learning environments.

- Treat students, parents, and colleagues with courtesy and respect.

- Hold students, parents, and each other to the highest standards of performance.

- Collaborate regularly with colleagues to seek and implement more effective strategies for helping each child to achieve his or her academic potential.

- Do whatever it takes—go the extra mile—to ensure that every student achieves or exceeds grade-level academic expectations.

Finally, even though the students they served included some of the most economically disadvantaged in their traditionally high-performing school district, the staff boldly proclaimed their intent to make their school one of the highest achieving in the district.

Achieving at High Levels With the Student Success Team

Like every faculty that sets their collective sight on ensuring all students achieve at high levels, the Los Pen staff soon faced the inescapable question, "What are we prepared to do when our students do not learn?" The Student Success Team (SST) became an important vehicle for answering that question.

The SST process is designed to assist classroom teachers in identifying interventions and developing solutions when a student is experiencing academic, social, or emotional difficulties. The team itself is composed of 6 to 10 staff members, one of whom serves as the SST coordinator and receives a small stipend for assuming the responsibilities. The coordinator is a teacher who serves as the data clerk of the team and coordinates and handles all referrals and paperwork. Six to eight additional teachers serve as SST facilitators—the staff members responsible for leading SST meetings. Facilitators are paid hourly and are selected for their expertise. One might have a gift for finding literacy strategies that lead a student to success, while another has an exceptional ability to support students with discipline issues. Each grade level has a representative that serves as a facilitator.

The SST process begins when a teacher refers a student to the team for consideration after all interventions available to the classroom teacher—differentiated instruction, collaborating with colleagues from the grade-level team, and conferencing with parents—have failed to bring about the desired improvement. Once each month, the SST coordinator convenes a meeting of all facilitators for the review of all referrals that have been received since the previous meeting. Each referral includes a listing of interventions the teacher has used, the dates of conferences with parents, and the goals the teacher would like to accomplish as a result of the referral. As the coordinator summarizes each referral, the entire team discusses which facilitator would be the best person to manage that particular case. The meeting concludes when all cases have been assigned to a facilitator.

Soon thereafter, the coordinator sets a date for a meeting between the facilitator, teacher, student, and parents and informs all parties regarding the logistics of the meeting. At this meeting the facilitator keeps detailed notes on an overhead transparency so that everyone at the meeting can see points of agreement regarding necessary interventions. A follow-up meeting is then scheduled within 6 to 8 weeks to assess the impact of the new plan of assistance for the student. The SST coordinator then enters the specific interventions that were agreed upon at the meeting into a database that the school uses to track the effectiveness of different intervention strategies.

Comprehensive Interventions

One of the most unique aspects of the Los Pen SST process is the attention that is paid to developing a comprehensive list of interventions. As Damen Lopez, principal of Los Pen, reasons, "If you can't supply SST facilitators with meaningful interventions, then the process is doomed. It's like sending soldiers into battle without ammunition. We needed to arm ourselves more effectively if we wanted to win the war of helping all students learn."

Over time, the staff was able to compile a comprehensive list of interventions, the focus of the intervention, and how each would be funded.

Los Peñasquitos Elementary Comprehensive List of Interventions

Impact Teacher Groups

These groups focus on teaching reading, writing, and math to small groups of 4 to 6 students. They are designed to give students extra time and support for learning in a small-group setting. A credentialed teacher provides instruction for 30- to 45-minute sessions. The program ensures that students who are experiencing difficulty are provided a "second helping" of instruction based on the philosophy that some students require more time to achieve the intended standard. Title One money is used to pay for hourly teaching from credentialed teachers.

Math Booster Clubs

These clubs offer extra support before school that focuses on basic math skills. Classroom teachers provide the instruction and are paid hourly through promotion/intervention funds available to all schools in California.

After-School Tutoring Clubs

These groups offer extra literacy and homework support to students after school. The classroom teachers who run this program are paid hourly through promotion/intervention funds available to all schools in California.

The Los Pen 6-to-6 Program

This program offers extra support from 6:00 a.m. to 6:00 p.m. and is funded through a city grant. It emphasizes character education and has been particularly helpful for students with behavior issues. The program serves 120 students every day. The 75 students on a waiting list to participate in the program are a testament to its success. Los Pen started the first 6-to-6 program in the district. The program has now been replicated and implemented in three other schools.

Counseling

A school counselor is available 2 days a week to support students with social and emotional concerns. Individual and small group sessions are available for students. If a student needs extended support outside of the school day, a district-wide "Caring Connections" program will pay for several sessions of counseling. Counseling is funded through a state-wide grant.

Los Pen Parent University

This intervention is specifically designed for parents. The first course, "Developing Capable Young People," is based on the work of H. Stephen Glenn and is taught by the school counselor. It is paid for with Title I parent money.

Mentoring

Staff members volunteer to serve as mentors to designated students and attempt to establish meaningful, one-on-one relationships with those students. Mentors provide academic and emotional support based on the individual needs of their students. This intervention is staffed by volunteers.

Peer Tutoring

Peer tutoring comes in several forms. For example, fourth graders help first graders who need extra practice in reading. Peer tutoring is also provided through "Buddy Classrooms" and middle and high school students who come to help as well. This intervention is staffed by volunteers.

Senior Citizen Support

Los Pen has created partnerships with several senior programs. Seniors come on site to work with students on reading and writing. This intervention is staffed by volunteers.

Community Partnerships

Several community partners offer support to students. This support ranges from working with classes on science projects to working with classes on community outreach projects. Members of the Community Partnerships program have, on occasion, also been called upon to promote the success of individual students. This intervention is staffed by volunteers.

SST Facilitator Support

One of the goals of the SST facilitator is to develop a personal relationship with the student. Facilitators check in on students and teachers each week and look for ways to support them any way they can. The facilitator receives an hourly stipend.

Classroom Teacher Support

The classroom teachers at Los Pen know that they are ultimately responsible for achieving academic success for all students. Therefore, they go the extra mile to do whatever it takes to make this happen. Extra one-on-one time during the school day or after hours, the development of individual academic and behavior plans and contracts, and continued close partnerships with parents are all examples of how the teachers generate success. This is part of the job for all Los Pen teachers.

Student Services Teacher

A full-time teacher on special assignment supports the social and emotional needs of students. This teacher helps to generate behavior plans/contracts for students and checks in on a caseload of students several times a week. This added support is helpful to the teacher, student, and parent. This intervention is supported by Title I funding.

Creative Grouping

Los Pen refuses to accept the notion that success must be generated within the four walls of the "homeroom class." On a regular basis, teachers create rotations and creative groupings that promote success for all. For example, a student who is struggling in reading at the third-grade level may work in a small group in a second-grade classroom. This is part of the job for all Los Pen teachers.

Literacy Specialist Support

Like all schools in its district, Los Pen receives support from a reading specialist 2 days each week. The principal has also developed a creative schedule that provides time for a highly skilled kindergarten teacher to help with literacy. She supports students in kindergarten through grade 2, while the reading specialist works with grades 3 through 5. As a result, the school is able to provide more time to support students in reading and writing through small groups or one-on-one support. No extra funds are needed for this intervention, just creativity.

Reading Recovery

This program offers intensive one-on-one reading instruction for the lowest-performing 10% of first graders. The daily schedule for kindergarten teachers was specifically designed so that they could provide this service to first graders. The only cost associated with the program is training teachers in Reading Recovery.

The Los Pen SST Concept

The SST concept used at Los Pen differs from more traditional student assistance teams in several ways. First, it honors teachers' time. In many schools, a student assistance team is led by one individual who facilitates all meetings with other members of the team who are relegated to the role of passive participants. In contrast, each facilitator at Los Pen is assigned to specific SST meetings and is called upon to lead his or her meetings. As a result, no one is attending *all* meetings and each member of the SST typically devotes only 2 or 3 hours per month to the process. This "divide-and-conquer" approach reduces the caseload for facilitators who are able to have a greater impact on fewer students.

Another way in which the Los Pen approach differs from more traditional student assistance teams is that classroom teachers cannot simply deflect problems to the SST. They must demonstrate that they have exhausted all the intervention strategies that are available to them, and they must be full participants in the meetings that are intended to develop solutions.

Most importantly, the Los Pen SST approach does not merely represent a hoop through which to jump on the path to testing a student for special education. The attention the school has paid to finding meaningful interventions of additional time and support for students flows from the belief that the staff can find solutions to a student's lack of success *without* resorting to special education. At Los Pen, when a student struggles, teachers do not assume the student is incapable of learning, they look for ways to provide the time and support that lift students to success.

Focused School-Wide Goals

Like Boones Mill, Los Pen uses specific school-wide goals focused on student achievement to drive the work of the collaborative teams. The staff begins the goal-setting process by using data to build shared knowledge of trends in student achievement. Once a target area has been identified for the school and an improvement goal has been established, each team is called upon to develop an action plan to contribute to the attainment of that goal.

For example, the staff's analysis of the data at the end of the 2002–2003 school year led to the finding that 18% of the school's K–5 students did not meet proficiency levels in writing. This finding, in turn, led to the adoption of a school-wide SMART goal to increase the percentage of students attaining proficiency by 5%. The members of the second-grade team then used the school goal to establish the following target for their students:

> "All students will improve on-demand writing scores by 2 rubric points or reach a score of 10 by the post assessment. The indicator will be writing prompts scored in January and March as well as the pre- and post-assessments. Our target time is June of 2004."

Three times each year the entire faculty works in articulation meetings to examine assessment data to track the progress being made on school goals, identify needs, and identify next steps in addressing the needs of students. The key to this review is the staff's conviction that all assessment data should be *easily accessible and openly shared.*

The Los Peñasquitos Academy

The fundamental assumption that drives Los Pen—we can help all students achieve at high levels *if* we work together to develop strategies that provide them with extra time and support for learning—is also illustrated in the Los Peñasquitos Academy. This magnet program operates as a school within the school serving 128 fourth- and fifth-grade students of all abilities. There are no academic requirements to enroll in the academy, only the will and commitment from parents and students to adhere to contract stipulations. The Academy is specifically designed to ensure that all of its students "acquire the knowledge, skills, and character traits that are essential for success in rigorous high school programs and for admission to competitive universities." As the *San Diego Union-Tribune* reported:

> The diverse student enrollment in this special program includes low-income and English-language learners, but the focus is on where they are going, not where they came from. The academy's brochure notes that every student is expected to be successful, and excuses for marginal performance based on their background are unacceptable (Gonzalez, 2003).

Teachers in the program adopt the classic PLC position: Learning will be the constant—all kids will learn—and time and support will be the variables. Students make several commitments as they enter the program, including prompt and regular attendance from 7:55 a.m. to 4 p.m., instead of the traditional 8:55 to 3:10. They commit to asking questions as soon as they have difficulty understanding a concept, and they promise to complete their homework.

Teachers make commitments as well. They promise they will do "whatever it takes" to ensure all students learn. They provide both students and parents with cell phone numbers, insist that students call them any time between 6:00 a.m. and 9:00 p.m. if they are having difficulty completing homework, and promise to return calls promptly. They consistently convey the following message to the students: You will attain the high expectations we have set for you because we will teach you what it takes to be successful.

Parents are included in these mutual covenants. They promise to ensure that their children have good attendance, to check their homework each night, to communicate with teachers, and to hold their children accountable for their behavior.

One of the explicitly stated principles that guides the Academy is a "focus on results." As the program's brochure explains:

> The Los Pen Academy focuses relentlessly on results. All students are expected to achieve, and excuses are never made based upon demographics. Hard work, responsible behavior, and persistence are valued above perceptions of native ability. Student achievement, as measured by tests and other objective standards, is expected to significantly outperform district averages.

Academy students have risen to meet the high expectations established for this program. They dramatically outperform their peers in the district, county, and state on all measures of assessment.

Developing Powerful Commitments

Los Peñasquitos Elementary School has won the United States Department of Education's Blue Ribbon Award and has been designated as a California Distinguished School. What has been the key to its undeniable record of success? The language used in the mission, vision, commitments, and goals of

Los Peñasquitos Elementary School can be found in school documents throughout North America. There are other schools that promise that "all children will learn," because staff will do "whatever it takes" to help every student achieve "high expectations" with "no excuses" because of the demographics or backgrounds of the student population. What is unique about Los Pen is that the people who make up its staff have transformed those phrases into powerful commitments that they act upon and bring to life each day. Principal Damen Lopez emphasizes that the programs the school has established to meet the needs of students have resulted from deeply held convictions regarding the fundamental purpose of the school. As he puts it:

> "We are convinced that every student can and will achieve grade-level standards or above, and because of this conviction, every member of the Los Pen staff lives by a 'No Excuses, Whatever It Takes' philosophy. We believe we can create a school of learners who can achieve future goals that up to this point would have been but a distant dream: goals of being the first in their family to graduate from a university, goals of breaking the chain of a history of poverty, goals of entering a profession. It is the power of our *belief in the ability of every student to achieve success* that makes us strong."

Of course, students at Los Pen, like students everywhere, sometimes experience initial difficulty in mastering key concepts and skills. This has not, however, caused the staff to rethink their assumption that all students can be successful.

They remain convinced that all students can master the essential learning of their school, but they also recognize some will need additional time and support in order to do so. Fortunately for the students at Los Pen, their principal and teachers have worked collaboratively to ensure that every child receives that necessary time and support.

Chapter 8

Common Threads

"[Great organizations] simplify a complex world into a single organizing idea, a basic principle, or concept that unifies and guides everything. . . . [They] see what is essential, and ignore the rest."

—Jim Collins, 2001, p. 91

"The most extensive and systematic program of research on organizational power and influence has led to one vital lesson that all leaders should take to heart: the more people believe that they can influence and control the organization, the greater organizational effectiveness and member satisfaction will be. In other words, shared power results in higher levels of satisfaction and performance throughout the organization. It is the most significant of all the five practices of effective leaders."

—James Kouzes & Barry Posner, 1987, p. 10

The preceding chapters tell the stories of four very distinct schools. They represent different grade levels, different sizes, different geographical areas, different communities, and students from very different backgrounds. At first glance, they seem to have far more differences than commonalities; however, closer examination reveals that these schools are similar in many important ways. These schools share:

- Clarity of purpose

- Collaborative culture

- Collective inquiry into best practice and current reality

- Action orientation

- Commitment to continuous improvement

- Focus on results

- Strong principals who empower teachers

- Commitment to face adversity, conflict, and anxiety

- The same guiding phrase

Clarity of Purpose

Staff members in each of the schools are clear about and focused on the fundamental purpose of the school: high levels of learning for all students. There is no ambiguity and no hedging. There is no suggestion that all kids will learn *if* they are conscientious, responsible, attentive, developmentally ready, fluent in English, and come from homes with concerned parents who take an interest in their education. There is no hint that staff members believe they can help all kids learn *if* class sizes are reduced, more resources are made available, new textbooks are purchased, or more support staff are hired. In these four schools, staff members embrace the premise that the very reason the school exists is to help *all* of their students—all the boys and girls who come to them each day—acquire essential knowledge and skills given the current resources available to the school . . . period.

In his research on high-performing organizations, Jim Collins (2001) found that great organizations "simplify a complex world into a single organizing idea, a basic principle, or concept that unifies and guides everything" (p. 91). The Big Idea, or guiding principle, of schools that operate as PLCs is simple: The fundamental purpose of the school is to ensure high levels of learning for all students. Because the faculties in these four schools held that fundamental conviction in common, they developed a shared vision of the school they needed to create to help all kids learn, made collective commitments regarding what they were prepared to do to help all kids learn, and set goals and monitored data to assess the progress they were making in helping all kids learn. The point to understand, however, is that the journey to becoming a PLC begins with an honest assessment of our assumptions regarding the ability of students to learn and our responsibility to see to it that they do.

Collaborative Culture

Each of the four schools was designed to promote a collaborative culture by organizing teachers into teams and building time for them to meet in the routine schedule of the school. When asked what advice she would give principals who were trying to improve results in their schools, Freeport's Clara Sale-Davis was quick to respond: "Build a collaborative culture, maintain common planning time for teachers, and turn to your data." When Mike Schmoker (2001) interviewed Stevenson High School teachers to find the secret of the school's sustained success, he heard a consistent response: our collaborative teams. Boones Mill teachers cited the creation of a schedule that gave teachers time to collaborate with their teammates for 70 minutes each week as the catalyst that launched them on the road to becoming a PLC (*Video Journal*, 2001). Teachers at Los Pen considered working together so vital to their mission that they pledged to "collaborate regularly with colleagues to seek and implement more effective strategies for helping each child to achieve his or her academic potential."

The importance of providing the structures to support meaningful collaboration between teachers is difficult to overstate. As McLaughlin and Talbert (2001) concluded:

> Chorus and refrain in our study of teaching and our understanding of the conditions that support teachers' learning and change is the critical importance of professional discourse and inquiry. Opportunities for teachers to talk with colleagues about teaching, consider new ways of doing things, and hammer out shared understandings about goals were common across diverse environments where practices were rethought in ways that benefited both teachers and students. (pp. 131–132)

These principals did more than put teachers together in groups and hope good things would happen. As Fullan (2001) observes, "Collaborative cultures . . . are indeed powerful, but unless they are focusing on the right things they may end up being powerfully wrong" (p. 67). These principals ensured that the collaborative teams focused on *learning*. They created a systematic process in which teachers worked together interdependently to analyze and impact their practice in order to improve results for individual teachers, for the team, and for the school.

Collective Inquiry Into Best Practice and Current Reality

In each of the four schools, building shared knowledge was a critical step in finding common ground. Teachers were more likely to acknowledge the need for improvement when they jointly studied evidence of the strengths and weaknesses of their school. They were more likely to arrive at consensus on the most essential knowledge and skills students should acquire when together they analyzed and discussed state and national standards, district curriculum guides, and student achievement data. They were more likely to agree on the most effective instructional strategies when they worked together in examining results from their common assessments. Teachers in these schools certainly had disagreements and differences of opinion, but they were able to find common ground on critical questions because they engaged in collective study rather than simply sharing their opinions.

Action Orientation

Teachers and principals in most schools can reflect upon the school year each June and conclude that, once again, their school has been characterized by an "action orientation." They can point to the launching of new initiatives, the diverse professional training they have received, and their response to the myriad of directives that descended upon them from the central office as evidence of their often frenetic activity. As the Consortium on Productivity (1995) concluded:

The issue is not that individual teachers and schools do not innovate and change all the time. They do. The problem is with the kinds of change that occur in the education system, their fragile quality, and their random and idiosyncratic nature. (p. 23)

What distinguishes these four schools is not their "busyness," but the fact that their efforts were guided by what Michael Fullan has described as *coherence*—"the extent to which the school's programs for students and staff are coordinated, focused on learning goals, and sustained over a period of time" (p. 64). The unrelenting focus on the three critical questions helped these schools bring coherence to their efforts. Assessments became linked to common essential outcomes. Staff development became linked to specific skills teachers needed to help students achieve those outcomes. School and team goals became linked to results. These schools illustrate one of Fullan's findings: The shift from a focus on teaching to a focus on learning is a "powerful coherence-maker" (Fullan, 2001).

It is important to recognize the focus and coordination that guided the work of these schools, but it is equally important to understand that, ultimately, the teachers and principals were required to *act*. The process of changing the culture of any organization begins by changing the way in which the people of that organization behave (Bossidy & Charan, 2002). None of the four schools experienced gains in student achievement merely by writing a new vision statement or developing a strategic plan. These schools did not see improvement until staff members began to *act* differently. They worked collaboratively rather than working in isolation. They developed common assessments and applied consistent standards rather than acting autonomously. They changed instructional pacing and strategies based on new insights into pedagogical effectiveness. They recognized that, until they began to *act* differently, to *do* differently, there was little reason to expect different results. These schools were not characterized by studied, deliberate musings. They were places of action, experimentation, and a willingness to test ideas that seemed to hold potential for improving student achievement.

Commitment to Continuous Improvement

Each of the four schools has been recognized as an exemplary school, yet there is no evidence that any of them have elected to rest on their laurels. The perpetual disquiet and constant search for a better way that characterizes these schools results from the continuous improvement processes that are embedded in the routine practices of the school. Although each is attentive to celebrating the success of individuals, teams, and the school at large, the systems that are in place call upon every team and every teacher to identify and attack areas for improvement.

If a team analyzes student achievement data and discovers that a particular math concept is the most problematic for their students, the team discusses the issue, develops strategies for addressing the problem, implements the strategies in their classrooms, and gathers new information to assess the impact of the strategies on student achievement. If their efforts have been successful, they can (and should) celebrate the improvement, but they will also shift their efforts to identifying and addressing the next, most problematic concept. There will always be an area where students do "least well"—an area that can be targeted for improvement.

The creation of a PLC does not call for the completion of a series of tasks, but rather for a process of continuous improvement and perpetual renewal. It is a constant challenge that is never quite completely solved. Yet talk to the teachers in these four schools and they will tell you the PLC process is energizing rather than frustrating because month by month and year by year they see new evidence that their collective efforts do indeed have an impact on student learning. These teachers have a clear sense of purpose and a powerful sense of self-efficacy. They will attest to the fact that becoming a PLC is a wonderful journey, even if the journey has no final destination.

Focus on Results

Each of the four schools assesses the impact of its efforts and decisions on the basis of tangible results. When teachers in a school are truly focused on student learning as their primary mission, they inevitably seek valid methods to assess the extent and depth of that learning. The teachers in these four schools all found that frequent, locally developed common assessments were a vital resource in their efforts to assess student learning. Doug Reeves (2004) found that "schools with the greatest gains in student achievement consistently used common assessments" (p. 70). He contends that common assessments, collaboratively developed and scored by every teacher at a grade level, represent "the gold standard in educational accountability" because these assessments are used to "improve teaching and learning, not merely to evaluate students and schools" (pp. 114–115).

The teachers in the four schools featured in this book embraced data and information from their common assessments because the assessments provided timely and powerful insight into the learning of their students. They can attest to the fact that these assessments *for* learning give them greater power, individually and collectively, to meet the needs of their students. They do not denigrate data that suggest all is not well, nor do they blindly worship mean, modes, and medians. They have a healthy respect for information that can help them understand areas of strengths and weaknesses in the learning of their students because they are keenly interested in results.

A fixation on results will ultimately, inevitably, lead educators to immerse themselves in the question of "How will we respond when, despite our best efforts, our students experience difficulty in learning key concepts?" What is so striking about each of the four schools is that each has addressed this question so directly. Each has created systems to monitor students on a *timely* basis, but more importantly, each has developed a *systematic* process of *intervention* that provides students with additional time and support for learning. Furthermore, because they are committed to the success of each student, these schools do not simply offer time and support; they *direct* students to devote the time and avail themselves of the support that will lead to success.

Strong Principals Who Empower Teachers (Simultaneous Loose/Tight Leadership)

A comprehensive study of the restructuring movement in education led to two significant conclusions: first, a strong professional learning community was critical to gains in student achievement, and second the principals who led those learning communities were committed to empowering their teachers. As the study concluded:

"Leaders in schools with strong professional communities . . . delegated authority, developed collaborative decision-making processes, and stepped back from being the central problem solver. Instead they turned to the professional communities for critical decisions." (Louis, Kruse, & Marks, 1996, p. 193)

This description captures a key element of the leadership styles of the principals who built the learning communities in the four schools this book has considered. Leadership was widely distributed in each of the four schools. Each school had the benefit of a guiding coalition for its change process, and all of the schools made a conscious effort to give teams and individuals the authority and autonomy that is often reserved for the highest levels of leadership.

Stevenson's guiding coalition was an administrative team made up of the principal, assistant principals, and the chairperson of each department. The team met every day of the school year. At both Boones Mill and Los Peñasquitos, the implementation of the PLC process was led by a School Site Council made up of a teacher from each grade level as well as representatives of the parent community. In both elementary schools, all teachers also served on one of several school improvement committees. At Freeport, all teachers were members of one of six school-improvement cadres. The Campus Advisory Team, which included the chair and co-chair of each cadre, functioned as the leadership structure for the school.

Stevenson, Boones Mill, and Freeport extended leadership opportunities still further by designating a team leader for their course-specific, grade-level, and interdisciplinary teams.

Los Pen created an Assessment and Curriculum Committee that directed the school's process for clarifying essential outcomes and monitoring the learning of each student.

The collaborative team process in place in each of the schools was designed to encourage very fluid situational leadership. If the team discovered that one its members had special expertise in a particular content area, in teaching a concept, in developing effective assessments, or in meeting the needs of a particular kind of learner, that member would naturally assume temporary leadership based upon expertise, rather than on position, when the team focused on that topic.

Commitments to Face Adversity, Conflict, and Anxiety

The faculties of each of the four schools cited in the preceding chapters became enthusiastic advocates for the collaborative culture and systematic interventions that are so critical to the PLC concept. It is important to note, however, that in every case, the principals faced the challenge of one or more staff members who were either aggressively or passively resistant to the new direction of their school. In one case, a teacher refused to adhere to agreements regarding essential outcomes and pacing. In another, a teacher made it evident that he felt his teaching was superior to that of his colleagues, and therefore collaborating with them was a waste of his time. In one of the schools, a teacher was consistently absent from team meetings and was adept at presenting excuses for the absences. In the fourth school, a teacher consistently failed to fulfill her responsibilities when the team divided tasks among its members. The issues may have varied, but ultimately each principal became aware of the fact that the behavior of a staff member was undermining the work of his or her team.

The consistent way in which each principal dealt with this challenge offers important insights into leading the PLC process. In every case, the principal met with the teacher privately, stated concerns very directly, and identified the specific steps the teacher was to take to remedy the situation. Finally, the principal asked how he or she might help the teacher make the necessary changes. The teachers did not always respond positively to these discussions. In some of the situations the teachers became quite emotional and defensive. The principals, however, did not hedge. They made it clear that the current behavior was unacceptable and that the need for change was imperative. They did so without rancor, but they left no room for doubt regarding their expectations. Sale-Davis even went so far as to hand out transfer requests to all her staff, encouraging them to apply for a transfer if they were unwilling to embrace the ideas of consistent learning outcomes, common assessments, and a collaborative culture. The faculty came to understand that the school stood for certain principles that every staff member was expected to honor.

Perhaps there are schools that have made the transition to a PLC without conflict or anxiety, but we are unaware of any. Disagreements and tension are to be expected. The question schools must face is not, "How can we eliminate all potential for conflict as we go through this process?" but rather, "How will we react when we are immersed in the conflict that accompanies significant change?" In *Crucial Conversations* (Patterson, Grenny, McMillan, & Switzler, 2002) the authors contrast how teams respond when faced with conflict. Ineffective teams will ignore the problem, letting it fester and build until resentment and frustration lead to an explosion of accusations and recrimination. Good teams will take the matter to the boss and ask that he or she deal with the problem and find a satisfactory solution. Great teams deal with the issue themselves, engaging in open dialogue and applying positive peer pressure to bring about the desired change.

The problem in schools is that teams almost never start out as great teams. Before they can get to the point where team members can work together to resolve the matter, it is likely that they will need the "boss" or principal to help remedy the situation. If, at that critical moment, the staff observes their principal is unwilling to confront obvious violations of PLC concepts, the initiative will soon begin to unravel. The norms of behavior for any organization are shaped by what the leaders tolerate (Bossidy & Charan, 2002). Principals must place a higher priority on promoting PLC concepts than on "getting along" with staff or avoiding conflict.

Thus, creating a PLC presents an interesting paradox for principals who hope to lead the process. On the one hand, they must disperse rather than hoard power because "shared or 'distributive leadership' brings the learning community together in a common commitment and shared responsibility for sustaining improvement" (National Commission on Teaching, 2003, p. 17). Unless teachers feel that they have a voice in the improvement process, they will view change as something that is done *to* them rather than *by* them. Most teachers will be unwilling to accept responsibility for the success or failure of the initiative unless they have had some authority in making key decisions and some discretion in implementing those decisions.

The ability of the principal to foster widespread leadership in the PLC initiative will play a major role in determining whether or not the initiative is sustained. Unless teachers come to embrace PLC concepts, the PLC process will always depend on the energy and tenure of the principal. When, however, the concept is owned by the entire staff, the school can endure changes in key leadership positions without missing a beat.

In all of the schools except Freeport, the principal who helped the staff launch the Professional Learning Community journey has left the school. The PLC concept, however, continues to thrive in those schools. The ability of the principals to encourage widespread leadership and shared responsibility helped drive PLC concepts so deep into the culture of the school that the process survived their departure. The transformation in the schools was the result of the altered assumptions, beliefs, expectations, and practices of the staff rather than the result of a single charismatic champion. A study of Stevenson High School illustrates the point. The author of that study concluded that the school had "built a culture of learning that is far more enduring than a shrine to a single man and his ideas. The vision and beliefs that make Stevenson High School what it is today are deeply embedded in the daily practices of its teachers, counselors, and administrators" (Richardson, 2004, p. 115).

On the other hand, at the same time that they are encouraging autonomy and discretion, principals must insist on adherence to certain tenets that are essential to the PLC concept and make it clear that teacher autonomy does not extend to disregarding those tenets. When Damen Lopez became the principal of Los Peñasquitos several years after the school had begun the journey, he surveyed the staff to identify the most important thing he could do as the new principal to sustain their PLC. The most consistent response he received was, "hold us accountable." His staff was right.

As Peter Drucker (1996, p. xiv) wrote, "Leaders . . . delegate a good many things; they have to or they drown in trivia. But they don't delegate the one thing that they can do that will truly make a difference, the one thing they want to be remembered for. They do it." Principals who hope to lead learning communities must be unequivocal champions, promoters, and protectors of key PLC concepts, and that is not a job they can delegate to someone else.

In our earlier work we refer to this paradox of strong and forceful principals empowering teachers as "simultaneous loose/tight properties" (DuFour & Eaker, 1998). Those who become skilled in this approach to leadership clarify the core concepts of the organization for its members, concepts that are sacred and not to be violated. At the same time, however, they give those within the organization tremendous autonomy in applying those concepts on a day-to-day basis. These leaders encourage freedom within parameters—"an ethic of entrepreneurship within a culture of discipline" (Collins, 2001, p. 124).

The Same Guiding Phrase

One of the most striking consistencies among the four schools is their use of the same phrase. When questioning the principals and teachers of these schools regarding the strategies of intervention to help all students learn, they inevitably provide the same answer: "We do whatever it takes." Unlike most schools, these schools have a plan for responding to a student who experiences difficulty in mastering key concepts. Furthermore, in these schools, the plan does not end with one or two steps. If Plan A does not work, there is a Plan B, and a Plan C, and so on. There are a series of steps that are taken on behalf of any student, in any class, whenever that student struggles. Although the details of the plans vary in the schools we have described, the final step of the plan is the same for all four: "**Whatever it takes.**"

Chapter 9

The Philosophical Challenges
to Systematic Interventions for Students

"Change zealots tend to demonize resisters, but
they are not really bad people. Like all of us, they
are a product of their history. They have had
experiences that have led to the adoption of certain deeply ingrained behaviors and habits. . . .
The best solution is usually honest dialogue."

—John Kotter, 1996, pp. 112–113

This book has argued that if schools are to fulfill their
mission of helping all students learn at high levels, they
must monitor each student's learning on a timely basis
and create procedures to ensure that students receive additional time and support when they experience difficulty in learning.
It has also contended that this time and support should be provided in a systematic way rather than left to the discretion of
individual teachers, that the system should include a number
of interventions based on increasing levels of support, and that
students should be directed rather than invited to avail themselves of the support system. We recognize that this proposal

will generate significant reservation on the part of some educators. We also recognize that those reservations are often based on serious and valid questions about what is best for students. Therefore, this chapter will examine and respond to the questions that are likely to emerge as a staff considers the implications of creating their version of a system of interventions for students.

Creating a System of Interventions

Question One: Doesn't this system of interventions simply enable students to act irresponsibly?

We want our students to learn more than content. One of our most important goals is that students learn responsibility, and this system is at cross-purposes with that goal. It calls upon us to take on more responsibility for student learning rather than placing the burden where it belongs—with the student. If we come swooping in to solve their problems by offering increasing levels of time and support when they have not done what is necessary to be successful, we are simply enabling and reinforcing irresponsible behavior. Students must learn there are consequences for failing to act responsibly. We deprive them of the opportunity to learn if we shield them from those consequences.

Educators can readily agree that it would indeed be preferable if every student who entered a school had the prerequisite knowledge, skills, and disposition to be successful. They are even quicker to agree that, unfortunately, many students lack one or more of those prerequisites. The disagreement comes from their views on the best strategy for responding to these students.

For example, algebra has been described as the definitive course for sorting and selecting students—the window of opportunity through which a student must pass in order to gain access to higher education. Some states have mandated that every student who enters high school should have already mastered algebra or, at an absolute minimum, should have the essential mathematical skills to be successful in a high school algebra course. Unfortunately, mandates not withstanding, many students do not. One way to respond to this problem is to proceed with teaching the mathematics curriculum as prescribed, repeatedly failing those students who did not acquire the necessary knowledge base prior to the course. Another strategy would be to identify the students who lack the prerequisite skills essential for their success and then provide them with additional time and support until they master the skills essential to success in algebra.

In assessing the merits of these competing strategies, a school must return to the question, "What is our fundamental purpose?" If the priority of the school is to punish students for not learning what they were expected to learn when they were expected to learn it, the strategy of perpetuating failure would be particularly effective. If the purpose of the school is to help all students achieve high levels of learning, the strategy would be counterproductive.

Students also benefit from self-discipline, a strong work ethic, the ability to manage their time in order to meet deadlines, and a host of other qualities that might come under the general heading of personal responsibility. The members of a staff can hope that every child will possess these qualities when he or she enrolls in their school, but they are likely to discover that many students do not. What is the best way to respond to those students?

Consider two very different schools. The staff of the first school exhorts students to study for tests, complete their homework on time, and persevere if they experience initial difficulty. But some of their students elect to ignore these admonitions. Teachers then impose a penalty—a failing grade or zeros on missed assignments. In effect, students are free to opt for the penalty rather than do the work. The second school offers no such option. If students do not put sufficient time into their studies, the staff requires them to spend time in a tutorial situation. If students do not complete their homework, they are placed in an environment where completion of homework is carefully monitored. This school strives to teach students responsibility by insisting students act responsibly—even if under duress—in the hope that students will ultimately internalize the lesson. Which of these schools is holding students accountable? Which has enabled irresponsible behavior?

Advocating for a Pyramid of Interventions is not the same as saying that students should not experience consequences for lack of effort or irresponsible behavior. It is reasonable to provide students with incentives for completing their work on time and consequences for failing to meet deadlines. A school that made learning its primary focus, however, would never consider absolving the student of the responsibility for completing an assignment as an appropriate consequence—particularly if the assignment was given with the assumption that it would promote student learning.

Los Peñasquitos Elementary School serves as an excellent example. Students there are no more innately predisposed to complete their homework than students in other elementary schools. But the fourth and fifth graders of the Los Pen Academy have a homework completion rate of 99% because teachers *insist* that students complete their homework each day. Teachers accept no excuses, and students learn they can either complete their homework when assigned or they can complete it during lunch while their friends are enjoying social time. Rather than complaining that 9- and 10-year-olds are not responsible, Los Pen staff members teach their students responsibility. The results they achieve speak for themselves. California attempts to assess the academic performance and progress of each school in the state. It then compares the performance of schools with similar demographics, assigning each school into one of ten categories with one being the lowest and ten being the highest. Los Pen earns the top ranking. Los Pen is a ten—in more ways than one!

When schools make working and learning optional, both students and teachers can take the easy way out. Conversely, when schools create a system of interventions similar to what has been described in this book, students are held accountable. Their schools bombard them with the message that "We will not let you off the hook. We will see to it that you do what is necessary to be successful. We won't place you in a less rigorous curriculum, nor will we lower our standards for this course or grade level. We will give you the support, time, and structure to help you be successful, but we will not lower the bar." This approach is the antithesis of "enabling."

Question Two: Are we forgetting the whole child?

All of this attention to academic achievement is a case of misplaced priorities. We need to address the needs of the "whole" child. What about their emotional needs? What about their artistic side? What about developing their character? This is just another example of the fixation with test scores and trying to reduce a child to a statistic.

In *Built to Last: Successful Habits of Visionary Companies,* Jim Collins and Jerry Porras (1994) identified the characteristics and qualities that differentiated organizations that were able to sustain high performance from their less successful counterparts. They discovered that ineffective organizations succumbed to the "Tyranny of Or" while their extraordinary counterparts embraced the "Genius of And." Low-performing companies created false dichotomies: "We must be either this or that, but we cannot be both." High performers recognized that such perceptions were needlessly limiting and, instead of choosing between A *or* B, figured out ways to have both A *and* B. As they wrote:

> We're not talking about mere balance here. Balance implies going to the midpoint, fifty-fifty, half and half. . . . A highly visionary company does not want to blend yin and yang into a gray, indistinguishable circle that is neither highly yin nor highly yang; it aims to be distinctly yin *and* yang—*both* at the same time, all the time. (pp. 44–45)

Schools are particularly prone to the "Tyranny of Or." Educators often assume they must choose between strong administrators *or* autonomous teachers, phonics *or* whole language, emphasis on core curriculum *or* commitment to the Arts, leadership anchored in the central office *or* site-based management, and so on. One of the most damaging examples of the "Tyranny of Or" is the belief that a focus on academics results in indifference to all of the other factors that constitute the well-being of a student.

For example, many educators contend that a commitment to student success in the core curriculum must come at the expense of the electives program. Although Stevenson has an enviable record of extraordinary academic achievement, its students have also won recognition for their accomplishments beyond the core curriculum. Stevenson's art program has been selected as the best in the state of Illinois, and in 1997 Stevenson was one of eight schools in the nation to receive an award from the United States Department of Education for Excellence in the Fine Arts.

Other educators express concern that an academic focus will deprive students of the joy of school. When the staff of Stevenson High School committed to take the school motto, "Success for Every Student" literally, they were ultimately drawn to the question, "What do we mean by success?" There was general agreement that successful students would be able to pass their classes and meet proficiency standards on a variety of academic indicators. There was also, however, general agreement that the ultimate success of a student was dependent on more than course grades or scores on a test. A task force comprised of staff, community members, and students delved into the question and concluded "successful" students would also assume responsibility for their own learning, demonstrate the self-discipline to set and achieve goals, participate fully in the life of their community, and a variety of other factors that came under the heading of personal and emotional growth. This Task Force on Student Success ultimately presented the Board of Education with both a list of the factors that should be considered and potential indicators that the school should monitor. Every year since, the school has presented an annual report that tracks the wide-ranging factors used to assess the success of its students. The annual report includes the results of a survey taken by every student in the school, as well as a survey of randomly selected representative graduates 1 year and 5 years after their graduation. These surveys have been instrumental in monitoring some of the factors the school uses to assess the "whole" child.

The annual survey conducted of all students in 2003 revealed that 95% of students reported satisfactory experiences with the co-curricular program and almost two-thirds felt they had played a leadership role within the school. Seventy-five percent of Stevenson students were actively involved in community service. The Student Council won the United Way Award for Community Service. Stevenson students have created and sustained an annual Holiday Give-A-Thon that includes over 90% of the students and staff. Since 1985 that initiative has assisted almost 4,000 families and nearly 20,000 individuals with food and gifts valued at more than one million dollars. The largest club in the school is dedicated to community service and provides over 2,000 hours of service each year. Every week Stevenson students volunteer to work at daycare centers, nursing homes, a food shelter, and a residence for adults with special needs. They are part of the Big Brothers/Big Sisters mentoring program, and they tutor elementary school children in after-school reading programs. Stevenson students make a significant contribution to local government as well. They conduct voter registration drives three times each year and serve as election judges in local, state, and national elections.

Thomas Lickona (2004), director of the Center for Respect and Responsibility and noted author on character education, calls for educators to create "schools of character," which he describes as:

> A community of virtue, a place where moral and intellectual qualities such as good judgment, best effort, respect, kindness, honesty, service, and citizenship are modeled, upheld, celebrated, and practiced in every part of the school's life—from the examples of the adults to the relationship among peers, the handling of discipline, the content of the curriculum, the rigor of academic standards, the ethos of the environment, the conduct of extracurricular activities, and the involvement of parents. (p. 219)

Lickona recommends three resources to help educators create such schools, and *Professional Learning Communities at Work* (1998) is one of those resources. Clearly he does not believe that the PLC's commitment to the academic achievement of students interferes with the development of the "whole child."

When the National Forum to Accelerate Middle-Grades Reform identified schools that could serve as models of effective middle schools, it considered more than test scores. These model schools also were assessed on the basis of their ability to create a personalized environment to support each student's social and emotional development as well as academic growth. The Forum sought schools characterized by stable, close, and mutually respectful relationships. Freeport Intermediate School was lauded as a school where "relationships are warm and caring, in a personalized environment. Students and parents like the school" (Schools to Watch, 2004c). An *Education Week* reporter who visited Freeport concluded that "teachers bend over backwards for students, whether that means accompanying them to academic competitions at their own expense on weekends or dressing up in wacky costumes to cheer them on academically" (Bradley, 2000).

Freeport's principal Clara Sale-Davis has made her mantra, "it's all about relationships," a guiding force of the school. She attributes Freeport's success to more than a focus on academics. As she puts it:

> "If the relationship isn't right between the teacher and the student, you can reform until the cows come home but transformation won't take place. We have been successful because children here feel our love and caring, in and beyond the classroom."

Contending that the PLC's commitment to the academic success of each student will result in indifference to the personal development of students is to fall victim to the "Tyranny of Or." If schools embrace the "Power of And," they can create a culture that fosters the development of students in all areas.

Question Three: But aren't we neglecting the gifted and high-achieving children?

Focusing all this attention on needy, lazy, or low-performing kids deprives our more gifted students of the resources and time essential to their development.

The assumption behind this challenge is that schools have finite resources and energy, and therefore addressing the needs of a particular group of students means the school is not addressing the needs of others. This is often the assumption that drives the initiatives of parents who believe their children are gifted and therefore should have access to curriculum and teachers that will both challenge and stretch them at the same time that it supports and nurtures them. The PLC model is based on the premise that all students benefit when placed in a challenging and supportive environment. The staff of a PLC attempts to create a culture that stretches all students beyond their comfort zone and then provides the support to help them be successful in meeting the challenge. Students who have become comfortable in self-contained special education classes or remedial classes are called upon to meet the challenge of the standard curriculum. Students comfortable in the standard curriculum are called upon to stretch to meet the challenges of the accelerated or gifted curriculum. Students in the gifted curriculum are challenged to see how far they can go in extending their learning.

One of the consistent messages students convey in surveys of their schooling experience is that their schools fail to challenge them. PLCs intentionally push students beyond their comfort zone and constantly convey the message that "You have the potential to do more than you have ever thought possible, and we are here to help and support you as you work to realize that potential."

Both collaborative teams and systems of intervention support this stretch culture. When teachers work together to become so skillful in teaching a particular concept that even students who typically have difficulty can understand that concept, all students benefit. When students of all abilities have a place to turn to for extra time and support if they experience initial difficulty in learning, all students benefit. The adage "A rising tide lifts all boats" applies to the PLC concept. A school culture that both stretches and supports students is a good place for all kids.

Once again, Stevenson High School can illustrate that point. In the early 1980s, Stevenson's Honor Program catered to a very select group of students. Students were required to score in the top 10% of their class on a nationally normed test as incoming freshmen to be eligible to enroll in an honor course. This highly exclusive program gave a very limited number of students access to the national Advanced Placement program. In 1985, 88 Stevenson students wrote a total of 133 Advanced Placement exams, with 83% of those exams earning honor grades. Over the years, as teachers worked together in teams to discover more effective ways of teaching, and as the school created structures to give students extra time and support for learning, teachers became more confident of their ability to help students meet the rigorous challenges of the Advanced Placement curriculum. Students were encouraged but not required to accept the challenge of the AP program, and encouraged but not required to write AP exams. By 2003 the number of participating students had grown from 1985's 88 students to 1,211 students and the number of exams from 133 to 2,754. Despite the fact that over 60% of the graduating class had written AP exams, the percentage of honor grades actually increased to 87%. This high percentage of success is not an aberration; the school has averaged 87% honor grades over the past 5 years.

No comprehensive high school in North America writes more AP exams than Stevenson, but providing access to a program that was once reserved for the academic elite has not adversely impacted the performance of the most capable students. The mode, or most frequent score, earned by Stevenson students in 2003 was five—the highest possible score—and no school has produced the single top AP scholar in Illinois more than Stevenson. The fact that the school is committed to the success of every student has not made it less effective in meeting the needs of high-performing students.

The tide has also risen for all students at Boones Mill Elementary School. As grade-level teams began to analyze common assessment results, not only did they initiate strategies and programs to respond to the students who needed more time and support, but they also became more responsive to the students who were ready for greater challenges. In essence, they were addressing a fourth corollary PLC question: How will we respond to students who have already learned it?

The time set aside for daily tutorial blocks also became an opportune time for teams to develop extension and enrichment activities for students. In other words, teams differentiated instruction—beyond anything a teacher working in isolation could ever do. Students who demonstrated proficiency on the essential skills and concepts were provided enrichment opportunities at the same time each day that some of their classmates received the additional time and support they needed to become proficient in the essentials. Because the flexible groups were formed on the basis of student performance on both math and language arts common assessments, a given student might need intervention in math, but enrichment in language arts or vice versa. Once a student was able to demonstrate proficiency after a period of intervention, he or she could be reassigned to an enrichment group.

Examples of enrichment activities at Boones Mill include centers-based instruction, individual or cooperative group research projects, computer-based tutorials or exploration, Junior Great Books reading circles, and integrated curriculum projects and presentations. Grade-level teams were assisted in this differentiation by the floating tutors, at least one special education assistant, volunteers, interns, and the gifted and talented coordinator, all of whom knew the exact time each day the team would be organizing students into these flexible groupings.

The results were incredible. In 3 years, Boones Mill tripled the number of students reaching "advanced proficiency" status (the highest level) on the state assessment in third grade language arts and doubled the percentage in third grade math. The number of students reaching advanced status in fifth grade increased by over 85% in both language arts and math. During the same 3-year period, the percentage of students scoring in the top quartile on state-mandated, nationally normed tests increased from 27% to 50%.

Freeport Intermediate School decided that *all* students would benefit from the inquiry-based discovery learning and higher-order thinking that characterizes gifted and talented education programs, so all of its teachers became certified as gifted and talented teachers. The chart below shows the growth in the percentage of students meeting the proficiency standard on the Texas Assessment of Academic Skills from 1995 to 2002.

Percent of Students Meeting the Proficiency Standard

Subject	Percent Proficient 1995	Percent Proficient 2002
Reading	69.9%	98.7%
Mathematics	55%	98.7%
Writing	72%	96.1%
Social Studies	56.9%	94.5%

This kind of improvement not only impacts low-performing students, it also changes the culture and expectations of an entire school.

Los Pen's commitment to helping *all* students reach their highest potential has benefited students of all abilities. The following charts demonstrate the increase in percentage of students scoring in the top quartile of a nationally normed achievement test and the decrease in the percentage of students in the lowest quartile during the first 5 years of the Los Pen commitment to the PLC concept.

Percent of Students Above the 75th Percentile

	Reading		Math		Language	
	1998	2002	1998	2002	1998	2002
Grade 2	25%	57%	45%	78%	42%	62%
Grade 3	21%	38%	43%	61%	21%	52%
Grade 4	33%	44%	30%	66%	29%	53%
Grade 5	31%	40%	39%	67%	32%	52%

Percent of Students Below the 25th Percentile

	Reading		Math		Language	
	1998	2002	1998	2002	1998	2002
Grade 2	22%	7%	14%	6%	19%	11%
Grade 3	25%	8%	15%	3%	23%	6%
Grade 4	22%	9%	22%	7%	18%	9%
Grade 5	18%	14%	18%	8%	21%	9%

Los Pen's attention to each student's learning not only moved students from the bottom quartile of this nationally normed test, it dramatically increased the number of students able to score in the top quartile of the nation. Los Pen's current principal, Damen Lopez, puts it this way:

> "One of the immediate perceptions placed on Title One schools like ours is that they focus only on the lowest performing students. While we as a school have a commitment to ensuring that every student meets or exceeds district and state standards, we do not ignore those students who are already meeting or exceeding standards. As our pledge says, 'We are committed to creating a school that knows no limits to the academic success of each student.' The two most important phrases in that pledge are 'no limits' and 'each student.' Because of this, our conversations as a school focus on one word: growth. Our commitment to moving all students towards standards is a given; however, it is our focus on growth for every student that ensures an exceptional education for all of our students. We strive to tap into the potential of every student and to take that student as far as he or she can go."

One key to becoming a PLC is a willingness to honestly assess the current reality of the school. An honest assessment of the data of each of the four schools highlighted in this book can only lead to one conclusion: A commitment to the success of every student benefits students of all abilities. A rising tide does indeed raise all boats.

Question Four: Isn't this what special education is designed to do?

This is just another version of special education. If the kids can't cut it, why not just put them in special education? That's why we have it.

Veteran educators will quickly acknowledge that student failure is often not a result of a disabling condition, but rather is a function of student indifference to school, unwillingness to do the work, or a host of personal problems that interfere with a student's ability to do what is necessary to be successful in school. If a school was able to identify every student who truly required special education services and did a wonderful job of providing those services, it would continue to face the harsh, cold reality that a number of its students were still not being successful.

Furthermore, in many schools special education has become a "first response" rather than a "last resort." Psychologist Abraham Maslow observed, "To a man whose only tool is a hammer, the whole world looks like a nail." If special education is the only significant intervention tool available in a school, it is inevitable that the school will come to rely upon that tool too frequently. A school with a multi-step system of interventions arms itself with a variety of tools for meeting the needs of its students and thus is more likely to find the appropriate strategy.

Boones Mill is an excellent example of this principle at work. Prior to building its system of interventions for students, individual classroom teachers worked diligently to help students meet the standards of their grade levels, but when students continued to lag far behind despite the best efforts of their teachers, the students would be recommended for special education. During the 1999–2000 school year, Boones Mill ranked first among the 11 elementary schools in Franklin County in the number of students referred for special education testing. In the 2000–2001 school year, the staff built its system of interventions that provided students with additional time and support for learning through a number of different strategies. As a result, the school went from referring the most students for special education to referring the least in a single year.

There are some very pragmatic reasons for looking for alternatives to special education. One is cost effectiveness. The combination of rigidly prescribed student-teacher ratios and the failure of Congress to fully fund special education legislation presents schools with a tremendous financial burden when attempting to fund their programs. A school-wide plan for intervention represents a savings to schools. A locally developed intervention plan is not bound by prescribed staffing levels. For example, Stevenson's Guided Study and Mentor programs are staffed at a 60 to 1 student-teacher ratio, but if those same students were placed in special education programs, the ratios would drop to no more than 20 to 1. Furthermore, every time an intervention is effective in helping students become successful in the regular education program, the school saves the expenses it would incur by placing that student in special education.

Another pragmatic reason for supplementing special education with systematic interventions is flexibility. The placement of a student in special education is typically cumbersome and time consuming. Schools are given 60 days to complete all that is required to designate a student for special education—staffing, parent consultations, testing, completion of profiles, and so on. Any subsequent change in the placement of a special education student will then require even more time-consuming procedures. But if timely, directive, and systematic interventions are in place in a school, a student can be shifted from one level of support to another within minutes, typically without the need for parent approval. For example, when students are assigned to mandatory tutoring at Stevenson, their parents are advised of the additional support, but the school does not seek their permission to provide it.

This flexibility also extends to the duration of services. It is not unusual for a student identified with a disabling condition in third grade to still be receiving special education services as a senior in high school. When a school has developed a system of interventions, the goal is to provide the services only until students demonstrate they are ready to assume greater responsibility for their learning. The focus is on gradually weaning the student from the extra time and support as the student becomes successful in classes. The interventions then serve as a safety net if the student should falter, but they are not intended to be a permanent crutch.

Freeport's Clara Sale-Davis contends that her school almost never recommends a student for special education. As she puts it, "If they have been in the regular program for 7 years, we are not going to suddenly conclude they need special education, but we are going to provide them with extra support. A child should not have to be labeled to get served."

Furthermore, Freeport is committed to educating special education students in mainstream classes. Its teachers have been trained to meet the needs of special learners because, as Sale-Davis puts it, "the best strategies for helping special education students master content help all students learn at higher levels."

In fact, Freeport has found that the more it includes special education students in mainstream classes, the higher the results they achieve as a school.

Special education serves a tremendously important role in a school committed to success for all students, but its services should be reserved for students who truly need them to address a disabling condition. When schools create a systematic process to provide additional time and support for students who experience initial difficulty in learning, all students can learn in "the least-restrictive environment" within a cost-effective and flexible framework. Special education is reserved for the purpose for which it was intended.

Building Shared Knowledge

Those who begin the PLC journey and the cultural shifts that it requires should not only anticipate but should also welcome challenges to PLC concepts. As Michael Fullan (1997) writes:

> Learning organizations will legitimize dissent. . . . The value of resisters has been missed. Trying to manipulate the change process to eliminate resistance is futile. A more successful process is listening to those who are resisting and seeking to understand what lies behind their resistance. (p. 223)

Challenges to PLC concepts provide leaders of the initiative with the opportunity to model the collective inquiry that characterizes a learning organization. Effective leaders will initiate dialogue, a process whereby participants seek to understand each other's perspectives, assumptions, and thought processes. They will advocate for their position and explain why they came to their conclusions, but they will also encourage others to question that position and will invite them to share the reasons behind their reservations. They will build shared knowledge with resisters in the belief that if people have access to the same pool of knowledge, they are more likely to arrive at the same conclusions.

Honoring the challenges of a resister and engaging in collective inquiry is not just a strategy for reaching consensus: it is a powerful tool for deepening one's own understanding of an issue. The benefits of PLC concepts will speak for themselves if educators demonstrate good faith toward one another as they honestly assess both best practices for helping all students achieve at high levels and the current reality of their own schools.

Chapter 10

Creating a Stretch Culture: A Process, Not a Program

"Probably the most important—and the most difficult—job of the school-based reformer is to change the prevailing culture of a school. . . . Ultimately, a school's culture has far more influence on life and learning in the schoolhouse than the state department of education, the superintendent, the school board, or even the principal can ever have."

—Roland Barth, 2001, p. 7

"Stretch goals need to be high enough to inspire extraordinary effort but can't appear so unreasonable or unattainable as to discourage people from reaching for them. Good stretch goals move people's focus from a determination to be as good as we *have* to be and asks instead, how good *can* we be."

—Noel Tichy, 1997, p. 143

Educators in search of the one new program that will transform their school may be tempted to view the development of systematic interventions for students as the solution to their problems. Unfortunately, the effect of simply adding programs to traditional school practices is neither significant nor lasting. The attention to interventions presented in this book should not be viewed as a program or add-on, but rather should be considered as part of the larger process of creating the culture of a Professional Learning Community. As Andy Hargreaves (2004) puts it, "Our work has demonstrated that a professional learning community is an ethos that infuses every single aspect of a school's operation. When a school becomes a professional learning community, everything in the school looks different than it did before" (p. 48).

School improvement initiatives have typically focused on the structure of the school—the programs, policies, procedures, rules, and hierarchical relationships that govern the school. Structural changes are appealing because they are so visible. A school district can point to tangible evidence of its efforts to improve when it raises graduation requirements, adopts a new homework policy, implements the block schedule in its high schools, or creates a new program. Developing a program of interventions in a school, although an essential step on the journey to becoming a Professional Learning Community, is only a structural change.

Unfortunately, structural changes have little lasting impact unless the changes ultimately become deeply rooted in the school's culture—the assumptions, beliefs, expectations, values, and habits that constitute the norm for that school. Culture has been defined as "the assumptions we don't see"

(Schein, 1992), "the stories we tell ourselves" (James, 1995), and "the way we do things around here." The culture of any organization shapes how people think, feel, and act. It explains their view of the world, reinforces their interpretation of events, and instructs them in appropriate conduct. The challenge of building a PLC goes far beyond the adoption of a program. A flurry of improvement initiatives will be for naught if those within the school fail to pay attention to shaping the culture. As Phil Schlechty (1996) advised, "Structural change that is not supported by cultural change will eventually be overwhelmed by the culture, for it is in the culture that any organization finds meaning and stability" (p. 136). The success or failure of the effort to build a PLC will depend on the ability of the people in the school to make some profound cultural shifts. The following text is not all-inclusive, but does represent some of the most essential cultural shifts schools should address.

Cultural Shifts for Developing the Culture of a Professional Learning Community

From a Focus on Teaching to a Focus on Learning

The single most important step a school will take on the journey to becoming a PLC will be the adoption of learning as the central purpose of the school. Traditional school cultures have focused on teaching. The prevalent question in those cultures has been, "What should teachers teach, and how should they teach it?" The PLC shifts the focus to the three critical questions presented throughout this book. It is virtually impossible to improve the achievement levels of large numbers of students across all abilities and backgrounds unless teachers are clear and consistent regarding what they expect students to learn in each course, grade level, and unit of instruction. It is also imperative that teachers frequently gather evidence of each student's learning through multiple forms of collaboratively developed assessments. Finally, the staff must develop a plan to identify students who experience initial difficulty in learning and provide those students with additional time and support for learning in a systematic way.

The pursuit of these questions flows from the conviction that the school exists not to provide students with a place in which they are taught, but rather to provide them with a place that ensures they learn. When educators come to embrace that purpose, and when they are willing to honestly confront the brutal facts about the current reality in their school, decisions about what to do and what to stop doing often become evident. All policies, programs, and practices are considered through the lens of "How does this impact student learning?" Those that encourage learning are embraced. Those that interfere with learning are discarded.

From Working in Isolation to Working Collaboratively

It should be evident that schools will never realize the fundamental purpose of helping all students achieve at high levels if the educators within them work in isolation. Schools can guarantee all students have access to the same essential outcomes only when the teachers in that school work together to clarify and commit to those outcomes. Schools can monitor the learning of each student on a timely basis and staff can identify the strengths and weaknesses in their own instruction only if teachers work together to develop common assessments, analyze the results, and assist one another with areas of concern. Schools can meet the needs of students who experience difficulty in learning only if staff members work together to build processes to provide those students with additional time and support in a systematic way. When collaboration focused on student learning becomes deeply embedded in the culture of a school, not only will students achieve at higher levels, but the school will develop higher quality solutions to problems; experience increased confidence among staff; expand the pool of ideas, methods, and materials available to each teacher; have the ability to test new ideas, and provide greater support for new teachers entering the school (Little, 1990). While the benefits of a collaborative culture have been cited repeatedly in research, there is no credible evidence that teacher isolation contributes to all students achieving at high levels. Once again, if a school becomes clear about and committed to the fundamental purpose of learning for all, decisions about what needs to be done become evident. Building a collaborative culture is a *sine qua non* of a PLC.

From Focusing on Activities to Focusing on Results

The culture of most schools honors activities rather than results. They point to the number of new programs that have been initiated, the thickness of the strategic planning document, and the variety of staff development activities that have been offered. Teachers are rewarded for activity—salary schedule credit for pursuing random graduate courses and continuing education units for attending unrelated professional workshops. A PLC, on the other hand, does not confuse activity with effectiveness. Instead, it continually challenges the people within the school to work together to answer the question, "What impact will this activity have on our fundamental purpose of learning for all?" The emphasis of staff development shifts from workshops to the workplace, from an external focus to learning in the setting where teachers work, from individual learning to group and organizational learning, and from a focus on activities to a focus on results. It is this organized, social learning in the context of the specific school setting that leads to improved results (Fullan, 2001).

From Fixed Time to Flexible Time

In traditional schools, time is a fixed resource. The length of the school day, the number of minutes per class, and the number of days in the school year are all rigidly set. When time is up, it is time to move on. In a PLC, time is considered a critical component in learning, and the school becomes resourceful in providing additional time for students who need it. If learning is to be the constant for all students, time must become a variable.

When a school makes a commitment to provide students with additional time for learning, staff members look for ways to make the school schedule a resource rather than a restriction. Often in our workshops participants will bemoan the fact that the schedule in their school will not allow them to provide students with additional support. We find that response puzzling. There are many things that educators are unable to change in their schools, but the schedule is not one of them. God did not create our schedules; we did! A school that contends it simply cannot find the time to help all students learn because of its restrictive schedule must ask, "What is the priority reflected in our current schedule? Is that priority truly more important than ensuring that students have time for extra support when they struggle?" Once again, if educators embrace learning for all as their fundamental purpose and absolute priority, and if they work together to focus their creative energy on the issue of time, they almost always discover they have the ability to create a schedule that supports rather than restricts student learning.

From Average Learning to Individual Learning

In traditional schools, averaging is a way of life. Teachers average grades. Schools are judged based on the average performance levels of students on state and national exams. If the fundamental purpose of the school was to ensure that on average our students learn, this reliance on averages would be very appropriate. But when a staff is committed to high levels of learning for *all* students, averages reveal very little. A PLC will monitor the learning of each individual student and intervene when that student experiences difficulty.

From Punitive to Positive

Many students hear the following message from their schools, particularly middle and high schools: "Here are our rules. Obey them or we will punish you." Ironically, very often the consequence for failure to adhere to the rules is denying students the opportunity to learn. We are familiar with a high school that proclaimed learning as its central purpose. The administration and faculty spoke eloquently about how important it was that students learn the course material. At the same time, the school had a policy that prohibited students from turning in assignments or doing make-up work if they had missed school with an unexcused absence. Suspension from school was considered an unexcused absence, and the leading cause of suspension was truancy. So the consequence for a student who cut a class was banishment from all classes and prohibition from completing assignments. A school that truly embraced learning as its fundamental purpose would certainly have applied a consequence for the unexcused absence, but excluding the student from the opportunity to learn and prohibiting the student from doing work that was designed to enhance learning would not be considered appropriate. In fact, that school would *require* the student to learn the material he or she missed during the absence. Furthermore, the school would look to create a system of incentives and privileges for students that would encourage them to attend to their learning and abide by rules essential to maintaining a safe and orderly environment. The school would think positive, not punitive.

From "Teacher Tell/Student Listen" to "Teacher Coaching/ Student Practice"

Much of what goes on in classrooms is based on a model of "teacher talk" and "student listen." It has been said that if a Martian were to observe a contemporary school and report his findings back on Mars, he would report that school is a place where adults come each day to work very, very hard, and children come to watch them work. Educators in a PLC understand that one of the keys to high levels of student learning is to design their classrooms and instruction to ensure that *students* do the work. They recognize that most of us learn by doing, so they set out to engage students in the learning process. They begin to view themselves not as dispensers of knowledge to passive participants but as coaches who guide students with clear direction, incremental steps, repeated practice, and immediate feedback as students work their way through the learning process.

From Recognizing the Elite to Creating Opportunity for Many Winners

Schools have always had ways to recognize individual students. It is not unusual for a school to have honor rolls, valedictorians, captains of athletic teams, or National Honor Societies. And in most schools, the overwhelming majority of students recognize from the very day they enter the school that they have no chance of ever receiving that recognition. When Peters and Waterman (1982) examined the characteristics of excellent organizations, they found these high performers shaped their culture by consciously developing systems to generate lots of winners and then celebrating individual and collective achievements. Schools should follow suit. It will be difficult to create a culture of success in a school that limits recognition of success to an elite few. When schools develop systems to honor not only the highest academic achievement, but also improvement, character, service, and persistence virtually all students can come to believe that school can be a place where they have the chance to be recognized and celebrated.

The Stretch Culture of a Professional Learning Community

As educators develop their capacity to function as a PLC, they create a culture that stretches the hopes, aspirations, and performance of students and adults alike. Students are encouraged to stretch beyond their comfort zone and pursue challenging curriculum. Teachers are stretched to develop and implement more effective strategies in their classrooms. The commitment to high levels of learning for all students and the focus on results stretch even the highest performing schools to strive for continuous improvement.

A stretch culture rests upon high expectations, which has been defined as the positive inferences teachers make about the future academic achievement of their students (Brophy & Good, 1980). For over a quarter of a century, a climate of high expectations for student achievement has been cited as a critical element in effective schools. Many schools, however, continue to misinterpret and misapply the findings of that research.

Some educators seem to adopt the position that they are demonstrating high expectations if they simply express their belief in the ability and self-worth of their students, surround students with positive affirmations, and make sure the students feel good about themselves. But a climate of high expectations requires more than cheerleading. Wishing happy thoughts or chanting "You can do it!" to students will have little impact on student achievement. In fact, if schools continue many of their traditional practices, there is little reason to believe that all students will learn at high levels.

A second misapplication of the research on high expectations is evident in the contemporary political climate in the United States. An assumption that drives many of the advocates of high standards for student learning is that if we merely raise the bar and demand more of students, they will rise to meet the new challenges. But demanding more of students without providing them additional support or expanding the skills of their teachers is unlikely to motivate students to reach higher. Rick Stiggins (2002) provides a much more likely scenario:

> Another huge segment of our student population, when confronted with an even tougher challenge than the one that it has already been failing at, will not redouble its efforts—a point

that most people are missing. These students will see both the new standards and the demand for higher test scores as unattainable for them, and they will give up in hopelessness. (p. 760)

By the fifth grade many students have learned to believe that their situation in school is hopeless. When failures pile up, when the bag of unlearned skills gets too large, students succumb to despair and look outside of the school for acceptance, success, and a sense of importance.

The concept of high expectations rests upon neither unwarranted optimism nor additional unsupported demands on students. It is not the perception of a staff regarding the ability of their *students* that is paramount in creating a culture of high expectations. The staff members' perception of their *own personal and collective ability* to help all students learn is far more critical. This belief in one's ability to impact the outcome on the basis of his or her personal efforts, or self-efficacy, is the cornerstone of a culture of high expectations.

The familiar tale of Professor Henry Higgins and Eliza Doolittle serves as somewhat of an analogy. Upon his initial encounter with the unschooled flower girl, Higgins makes a bold claim:

> You see this creature with her curbstone English: the English that will keep her in the gutter to the end of her days. Well, sir, in three months I could pass that girl off as a duchess at an ambassador's garden party. I could even get her a place as lady's maid or shop assistant, which requires better English. (Shaw, 1913, p. 18)

It was not his confidence in Eliza Doolittle that convinced Higgins he could help her achieve a very high standard; it was his confidence in himself. Now add to that sense of confidence the caring and compassion that characterize all great teachers, and we have an illustration of teacher self-efficacy that generates the high expectations for student achievement essential to a stretch culture. In such a culture, teachers can advise their students: "This unit will be challenging, but we can do this. We have learned how to help students just like you be successful in accomplishing things they never thought were possible. We believe in you, and if you believe in us and do what we ask of you, together we can meet this challenge."

It is not national legislation demanding that all students learn or the adoption of rigorous standards that will transform schools. In fact, in many schools the effort to raise standards and have tougher high-stakes assessments will not contribute to the creation of a stretch culture, but will instead contribute to a culture of learned hopelessness for students and staff alike. In other schools the standards movement will be used as a catalyst to help students achieve at higher levels. The staff of some schools will look for external solutions, waiting for the state to change legislation, the district to provide more resources, or the parents to send more capable students to their schools. They will look out the window for solutions. In other schools the staff will work together collaboratively to develop their collective capacity to meet the needs of their students. They will look in the mirror for solutions. Ultimately, what will make the difference is not the standards themselves, but the self-efficacy of the staff—their belief that it is within their sphere of influence to impact student achievement in a positive way.

Promoting Collective Self-Efficacy

If staff self-efficacy is the key to creating the stretch culture of a PLC, then one of the most pressing questions facing a school is, "What can we do to promote the belief in our ability to make a difference?" We concur with authors such as Milbrey McLaughlin and Joan Talbert, Rick Stiggins, Roland Barth, Mike Schmoker, Doug Reeves, Michael Fullan, Linda Darling-Hammond, and Fred Newmann who call upon teachers to build Professional Learning Communities—to work together to clarify essential student outcomes, gather timely evidence regarding student learning, and collaborate with one another to identify ways to address student weaknesses and build upon student strengths.

Rick Stiggins (2002) refers to this process as assessment *for* learning in contrast to summative state and national tests, which represent assessment *of* learning. He contends that teachers are engaged in assessment *for* learning when they work together to:

- Understand and articulate *in advance of teaching* the achievement targets that their students are to hit. (Answer the question, "What is it we want our students to know and be able to do as a result of this course, grade level, or unit?")

- Inform their students about those learning goals *in terms that students understand*, from the very beginning of the teaching and learning process.

- Develop assessment exercises and scoring procedures that *accurately reflect student achievement.* (Answer the question, "How will we know if each student has learned?")

- Use classroom assessments *to build students' confidence* in themselves as learners and help them take responsibility for their own learning, so as to lay a foundation for lifelong learning.

- Translate classroom assessment results into frequent *descriptive feedback* (versus judgmental feedback) for students that provides them with specific insights as to how to improve (such as helping students understand the criteria that will be used to judge the quality of their work).

- Continuously *adjust instruction* based on the results of classroom assessments. (Use formative assessments as the impetus for discussing, "How will we respond when our students experience difficulty in learning?")

- Engage students in *regular self-assessment* with standards held constant so that students can watch themselves grow over time and thus feel in charge of their own success (for example, train students to apply the criteria by which their work will be judged).

- Actively involve students in *communicating* with their teacher and their families about their achievement status and improvement.

This process will serve as a stimulus for greater teacher self-efficacy and higher levels of student achievement *only* if staff members work through it collaboratively. An individual teacher, working in isolation from colleagues, could engage in the steps described above and continue to get poor results due to ineffective instructional or assessment strategies. In fact, over time that teacher could use those poor results to draw erroneous conclusions about the ability of his or her students to learn.

But success stories can emerge when teachers work *together* to clarify outcomes, establish common formative assessments, gather frequent information on the achievement of their students and share their findings with one another. When a team of teachers suddenly discovers that one of their colleagues has been particularly successful in teaching a certain kind of student or a particular concept, it becomes more difficult for its members to contend that teachers cannot have an impact on student achievement. When teams throughout a school are setting and achieving SMART goals that raise student achievement to new levels, arguing that better results are impossible becomes more problematic. Two of the most significant steps a school can take to foster self-efficacy among staff are to stop the isolated, private practice of independent subcontractors and to insist on collaborative teams in which members share their practices and their results—successes as well as setbacks.

Everyone benefits when every teacher is able to get frequent feedback on the performance of his or her students in meeting an agreed-upon standard on a valid assessment in comparison to similar students in the school who are attempting to meet that same standard. When teachers are able to identify problem areas in the learning of their students, to find colleagues who have been more effective in addressing that area, and to lean into and learn from one another, a school has created fertile ground for the self-efficacy essential to PLCs. In working together, teachers can transform data and information into knowledge that can enhance the effectiveness of their practice. Fullan (2001) advises, "If you remember one thing about information, it is that it only becomes valuable in a social context." Or as Henry Louis Gates concludes, "Collecting data is only the first step toward wisdom, but sharing data is the beginning of community" (IBM, 2003).

But even when teachers work together in this powerful cycle of continuous improvement, there will be students who continue to experience difficulty in learning. If educators continue to assume that learning happens only in the classroom within the limits of fixed time and support, those students will continue to struggle. But when the members of a staff make a powerful paradigm shift, when they begin to create effective systems of intervention that ensure struggling students receive additional time and support, their collective sense of confidence in their ability to help all students will be enhanced.

Schools that attend to both strategies—building a collaborative culture that focuses on student learning and creating a system of timely interventions for students—experience a powerful synergy. To overlook either of these strategies lessens the likelihood that staff will accept responsibility for the learning of all students.

Building Momentum Through Short-Term Wins

Another strategy for fostering self-efficacy is translating PLC concepts into small steps and celebrating the attainment of each step. The process of becoming a PLC does not occur as a single, dramatic breakthrough or miracle moment. Instead, the process requires sustaining a consistent, coherent effort for an extended period of time. Jim Collins' (2001) description of organizations that made the leap from "good to great" also applies to schools that are able to make significant advancements on the PLC continuum. As he wrote:

Good to great transformations never happened in one fell swoop. There was no single defining action, no grand program, no one killer innovation, no solitary lucky break, and no wrenching revolution. Good to great comes by a cumulative process—step by step, action by action, decision by decision, turn by turn of the flywheel—that adds up to sustained and spectacular results. (p. 165)

Thus, while leaders need a few key big ideas to provide the conceptual framework and coherence essential to successful school improvement, it is equally imperative that they recognize the need for specific, short-term implementation steps to advance those ideas. They can paint an attractive picture of the desired future state of the school, but they must balance this futuristic vision of what the school is working toward with steps that can be taken today.

The implementation and celebration of small steps generate both a sense of self-efficacy for staff and the momentum essential for improvement initiatives. While it takes time to drive PLC concepts deep into the culture of a school, the effort will lose momentum if there is nothing to celebrate in the short term. Kouzes and Posner (1987) advise leaders to "break down big problems into small, doable steps . . . plan for small wins. Small wins form the basis for a consistent pattern of winning that appeals to people's desire to belong to a successful venture. . . . A series of small wins provides a foundation of stable building blocks for change" (pp. 218–219). Collins agrees that people need to see tangible, incremental results in order to build momentum, and Kotter (1996) warns that most people will not sustain an improvement initiative unless they see compelling evidence in its early stages that the effort is producing the intended results. Gary Hamel's advice to leaders is succinct: Win small, win early, win often (2000).

The principals who built the powerful PLCs presented in this book were effective in articulating the conceptual framework and the key guiding ideas for their schools. They were equally masterful in translating those big concepts into incremental steps. They did more than hope for short-term wins; they *planned* for short-term wins to sustain momentum. They established calendars that called for the completion of projects in weeks and months rather than years, and they helped teams establish interim goals as stepping stones to more ambitious stretch goals.

Completion of tasks and achievement of objectives will not, however, fuel momentum unless people in the school are made aware of the progress that is being made. The principals of the four highlighted schools recognized this fact, and each set out to make celebration a significant part of the culture of the school. Stevenson High School *never* has a faculty meeting without public recognition of and a collective ovation for the accomplishments of specific teams or the school in general. Every faculty meeting at Boones Mill Elementary School includes a "Share the Learning" celebration in which teams share key insights they have acquired that are having a positive impact upon their work. At the monthly staff meetings at Los Peñasquitos, the prior recipient of the "Whatever It Takes" award presents the award to a colleague who has demonstrated exceptional commitment to the school's vision and values. The celebrations often have an air of playfulness such as when

Clara Sales-Davis rode into a pep assembly at Freeport on a Harley-Davidson motorcycle to celebrate students meeting an academic challenge.

The Power of Stories

Jennifer James (1995) has described culture as "the stories we tell ourselves." Effective leaders recognize this fact and use stories to shape the culture of their organizations. The ability to engage people through vibrant stories has been described as "an essential prerequisite for becoming a first-class winning leader" (Tichy, 1997) and "the single most powerful weapon in the leader's literary arsenal" (Gardner, 1990).

The principals of the four schools utilized this powerful weapon at every opportunity. They viewed every meeting—from large-group faculty meetings to small-group dialogues, parent programs to public assemblies—as a forum for preaching the message that "we are achieving great things, we are becoming the school we hoped to become, because of our collective efforts." They bombarded staff members with consistent stories reminding them of their common purpose, the importance of their work, and their collective commitments. But they went beyond simple cheerleading to tell stories that presented proof of the school's success. They constantly sought and shared evidence of small-term wins and indicators of improving student achievement. They solicited and reported student and parent testimonials regarding teachers who had made a significant difference in the lives of students. They publicly acknowledged individuals and teams whose efforts demonstrated the vision and values of the school. It becomes very difficult to claim that educators have no impact on student learning when teachers are immersed in stories of goals not only met, but exceeded, of extraordinary accomplishments and commitments of their colleagues, of steadily rising student achievement, and anecdotal evidence that students and parents recognize teachers who have inspired a child, These principals promoted a palpable sense of self-efficacy among their entire staff because they were attentive to creating conditions for short-term wins and immersing teachers in a culture that celebrated those wins as evidence of the school's success.

Why Not Now?

One of the most powerful lessons we have learned in working with schools as they attempt to implement PLC concepts is that those who make the most progress are those who take action. Many schools have a tendency to procrastinate. They contend that before they can take the first steps on the journey to becoming a PLC they need more time to study, or more training, or the conversion of the last few resisters. We have seen no evidence that spending excessive time in preparation to become a PLC leads to greater success. In fact, we concur with Mike Schmoker (2004) who found a negative correlation between the time spent preparing and developing strategic plans and actual progress on the PLC journey. Teachers and principals who do the best job in learning what it takes to build a PLC are those who immerse themselves in the process. They act, they make mistakes, they learn from their mistakes, and then they begin again more intelligently.

Think of your own experience in preparing to enter the field of education. Most teachers spend 4 or 5 years taking courses in their subject areas, methods courses, and foundation courses. Yet virtually every teacher would acknowledge that they learned more about the real work of education in their first semester of teaching than in the years of preparing for it. We learn by doing, and schools that learn what it takes to become PLCs are those that are doing the work of PLCs. Don't wait for the stars to align perfectly, for just the right conditions, or for the support of the last staff members. No school ever completed this process flawlessly, and you are unlikely to be the first. JUST DO IT. As Steven Covey (2002) admonishes, "To *know* and not to *do* is really not to know" (p. xiv).

A Final Analogy

The movie *Apollo 13* (1995) tells the story of how the men and women of NASA responded to the crisis of a crippled spacecraft that threatened the lives of its three astronauts. Problems emerged that NASA engineers had never anticipated or simulated. They were being called upon to do things that had never been done before in the space program. Time was short as the oxygen in the spacecraft was rapidly depleting. Resources were few. In one powerful scene an engineer empties a box of varied materials on a table and announces that those materials are all that is available to the astronauts to correct the problem in their spacecraft. The world watched and waited to see how this drama would unfold.

How did NASA respond to this difficult, desperate situation? First, the leader of the NASA team called upon its members to recommit to the fundamental purpose of NASA—to send men into space *and return them safely to earth*. He emphatically told them, "Failure is not an option." He then called upon them to build greater collective knowledge than they ever had before regarding the capacity of the spacecraft. He insisted they contact every designer, technician, and engineer who had played a role in developing every component of the spacecraft to come to deeper understanding of its capabilities. Most importantly, the scientists and engineers of the NASA team did not retreat to their individual cubicles to search for solutions. They worked together collaboratively and built upon each other's insights and strengths. They did so because lives hung in the balance.

It is unlikely that Hollywood will make a movie about the efforts a school makes to meet the challenges confronting it, but in many ways those challenges are similar to the *Apollo 13* scenario. Educators are also being called upon to do something that has never been done before. They too face a difficult, even desperate situation. They too feel the pressure of not enough time to complete what they are asked to accomplish. They too are frustrated by a lack of adequate resources. So how will they respond?

Will educators recommit to their fundamental mission—to ensure high levels of learning for each student? Will they pronounce that "Failure is not an option," and mean it? Will they build shared knowledge and come to a deeper understanding of their craft? Will they work together collaboratively to address their problems and challenges because they know there is no hope of success if they work in isolation? Will they recognize that in a very real sense, lives are hanging in the balance? We urge them to do so, not for the sake of improved test scores, but for the sake of the dreams and aspirations of the children whose lives they touch.

Appendix

The following pages contain examples, handouts, letters, and assessment tools that can be used as schools extend their missions of "learning for all" to make sure that every student learns—whatever it takes.

This letter is sent from a Stevenson counselor to a teacher who has volunteered to take a special interest in a student assigned to his or her class. The letter explains the purpose of the program.

Stevenson counselors send this letter to parents of designated incoming freshmen in the spring of the students' eighth grade year. These students have been identified through the Counselor Watch dialogues as needing additional academic support as they enter high school. Survival Skills for High School is designed to help students acquire the study skills necessary for their success. Note that Stevenson offers a full array of summer school courses to all students and that it encourages parents of all entering freshmen to enroll their students in a summer school course. Over 80% of incoming freshmen take at least one course in the summer prior to high school, so there is no stigma attached to attending a summer school program. Note also that a foundation has been established to assist with the tuition cost for any student whose family is unable to pay the fee for the program.

This document explains the role of the faculty advisor and counselor in Stevenson's Freshman Mentor Program. This program provides all freshmen with a teacher, counselor, and upperclassman mentor to assist with their transition to high school, to monitor their academic performance, and to answer any questions they might have throughout their first year of high school.

This worksheet is completed by every entering Stevenson freshman within the first month of school. It is monitored by the advisor and counselor and reviewed with the student throughout the year. The goal sheet asks students to identify what they hope to accomplish in high school, and the ongoing review sends the message that the staff is available to encourage and assist them in realizing their goals.

This sheet is completed by all entering freshmen as they register for their courses in the spring prior to enrolling at Stevenson. It is intended to send the message that participation in co-curricular activities is an expectation rather than an invitation. Note that each student will receive a direct invitation from a coach or sponsor to attend the first meeting of the organization.

This document clarifies expectations for students who are about to enter the Guided Study Program at Stevenson, a program designed to ensure that students will complete all homework and develop the skills and dispositions to be successful in every class.

This document provides an overview of the strategies developed by the faculty at Boones Mill Elementary School to promote the success of every student. The principal and teachers are committed to implementing this comprehensive plan to clarify what each student is to learn, assess the learning of each student on a timely basis, provide additional time and support for students who experience difficulty, and create a school culture that promotes and celebrates the learning of students and staff.

This document is an example of how teachers at Boones Mill attempted to make parents partners in the learning process and to use parents as a source of additional time and support. Note that the document clarifies what students should know and be able to do as they enter fifth grade as well as the knowledge and skills students should acquire as a result of their fifth grade program. The document provides tips for parents and a series of questions they might use at home to reinforce student learning.

This document explains a program developed by Boones Mill staff to assign a caring adult to individual students in the school who need additional support. The document offers suggestions for initiating the relationship with the student and guidelines for working with the student.

This document was used at Boones Mill to provide ongoing, two-way communication between each grade-level team and the principal. Teams would complete the feedback sheet after their meeting each week and submit it to the principal. She in turn used the feedback sheet to monitor the work of the teams and to respond immediately to any questions or concerns that they listed.

The goal of a Professional Learning Community is to build a culture in which staff members collaborate on issues that will help students achieve at higher levels. The goal is not merely to collaborate, and in fact, much of what passes for collaboration in schools today is unlikely to have any impact on student achievement. Stevenson High School created the 15 critical questions to guide the work of its collaborative teaching teams. Each question calls upon the team to generate a product as its response to the issue that is being raised. The questions can be extremely helpful in focusing the work of teams, particularly if a staff works together to establish a timeline for considering each question and generating the product that responds to it.

The Professional Learning Community Continuum

It is helpful to view the development of a Professional Learning Community as a process that moves through stages rather than a dichotomy that stipulates a school is or is not a PLC. This document provides a tool for assessing a school's progress through four stages of the PLC continuum: pre-initiation, initiation, developing, and sustaining. The continuum is most helpful when a staff is willing to engage in an honest and candid assessment of their current reality and to cite examples and illustrations to support their conclusions.

Mission Statement

_____

Freeport Intermediate School

Freeport Intermediate School provides a positive learner-centered environment that fosters creativity, academic excellence, and lifelong learning.

Relationships: Forming the foundation for all school and community interactions.

Exemplary Performance: Ensuring equity and excellence for all students.

Diversity: Celebrating and honoring our multicultural society.

Spirit: Creating a unity of purpose through a spirit of cooperation and adventure.

Knowledge: Empowering each child to compete successfully in the 21st Century.

Innovation: Utilizing technology and creativity in all aspects of teaching and learning.

Network: Providing students connectivity in learning through student and teacher teams.

Success: Instilling pride and enthusiasm, which permeate the learning community.

Pledge Statements

Los Peñasquitos Elementary School
A California Distinguished and National Blue Ribbon School

Our Pledge

This document reflects the collaboration of the teachers, staff, and parents of Los Peñasquitos Elementary to define and state our mission, vision, shared commitment, and goals set on behalf of our students. If you feel that we are not living up to this pledge, please contact your child's teacher or the principal.

Our Mission

Because we believe that all students who have been in Poway schools for at least 1 year can meet or exceed the yearly exit standards of the Poway Unified School District, we are prepared to do everything in our ability to make this happen. Gifted and high-achieving students will be challenged to reach their academic potential regardless of grade level limitations. Special Education students will meet or exceed their Individual Education Plan goals. And English Language Learners will meet or exceed the State English Language Development Standards in Language Arts.

Everyone involved at Los Peñasquitos Elementary believes that the academic potential of each student is tremendous. We refuse to accept difficult challenges that confront some students as excuses for poor learning. We know that one of the greatest predictors of life success is educational success. Therefore, we are committed to creating a school that knows no limits to the academic success of each student.

Our Vision

Students at Los Peñasquitos Elementary will be the most academically successful students in the Poway Unified School District. English Language Learners (ELL), Special Education students, and all other students who have been in the Poway Unified School District for at least 1 year and who receive neither ELL nor special education services will lead the district in academic achievement when compared to other students in their group.

Our Shared Commitment

The teachers at Los Peñasquitos Elementary pledge to:

- Accept no limits on the learning potential of any child.

- Meet the individual learning needs of each child.

- Create serious classroom learning environments.

- Treat students, parents, and colleagues with courtesy and respect.

- Hold students, parents, and each other to the highest standards of performance.

- Collaborate regularly with colleagues to seek and implement more effective strategies for helping each child to achieve his or her academic potential.

- Do whatever it takes—go the extra mile—to ensure that every student achieves or exceeds grade level academic expectations.

Our Goals

At the end of each school year, the staff at Los Peñasquitos Elementary will examine data to appropriately compare the academic achievements of our students with those attending other elementary schools in the Poway Unified School District. It is our goal and our expectation that, by the year 2011, students at our school will be the highest performing students in the district. The measures of student learning that we will use for the 2002–2003 school year are Academic Performance Index (API) scores that will be computed by the State of California. These scores will be available in the fall of 2003.

By meeting the following target goal, students at Los Peñasquitos Elementary will be on track for accomplishing what few people thought possible:

> By the fall of 2003, Los Pen students will score within the top ten elementary schools in the Poway Unified School District based on API scores.

Academy Brochure for Parents

Los Peñasquitos Elementary School

Los Penasquitos Academy

FOUNDED 2000

14125 Cuca Street
San Diego, CA 92129

Phone: 858-672-3600
Fax: 858-672-4390

Contact person:
Damen Lopez, Principal

Web site:
http://powayusd.sdcoe.k12.ca.us/abayro

What is the Academy?

The Los Penasquitos Academy is part of Los Penasquitos Elementary School in the Poway Unified School District. We are the first magnet program in the history of PUSD. For the 2003-2004 school year we have openings for approximately 60 fourth graders and 15 fifth graders.

2002-2003 Los Pen Academy

Why the Academy?

- This is an opportunity for any family that is willing to work extremely hard, take personal responsibility, and show dedication to learning.
- More time is devoted to learning. Students are in class for an additional two hours each day, and the Academy school year begins on July 21st.
- Extremely high expectations for academic achievement, responsibility, and respectful behavior are part of the Academy culture.
- Academy teachers are extraordinarily committed to the success of their students. They each have cell phones provided by the school, and are on call six days a week between the hours of 6:00 a.m. and 9:00 p.m. for homework help or questions from parents.
- There is a strong focus on developing student work habits and attitudes that will lead to success in a university setting.
- An unusually strong sense of camaraderie and pride is felt among the students.

Five Pillars

High Expectations

The Academy has well defined, observable expectations for academic achievement and conduct. Every student is expected to be successful, and excuses for marginal performance that are based upon the background of the students are never accepted.

Choice and Commitment

Students, parents and teachers choose to be at this school. No one is forced to attend or participate. Everyone must make and uphold a commitment to the school and to each other, and agree to dedicate the time and effort necessary to achieve success.

More Time

There are no shortcuts when it comes to helping students to succeed academically. Academy students attend school 48% more hours than do students in traditional classes (1600 hours vs. 1080 hours).

Focus on Results

All students are expected to achieve, and excuses are never accepted. Hard work, responsible behavior, and persistence are valued above perceptions of native ability.

Authority to Lead

The principal of the school has substantial control over budget, curriculum and personnel issues. This is essential when providing leadership to a program that moves far beyond the status quo.

Academy Contract

TEACHER'S COMMITMENT
I fully commit to the Academy in the following ways:

- I will do whatever it takes for students to learn.
- Cell phone messages may be left at any time, and I will return messages between the hours of 6:00 a.m. and 9:00 p.m. Sunday through Friday.
- I will always protect the safety, interests and rights of all individuals at the Academy.

PARENTS'/GUARDIANS' COMMITMENT
We fully commit to the Academy in the following ways:

- We will make sure that our child arrives to the Academy by 7:55 a.m. and stays until 4:00 p.m. every day. School begins on July 21, 2003 and ends on June 17, 2004.
- We will do whatever it takes for our child to learn.
- We will check our child's homework every night, let him/her call the teacher if there is a problem with the homework, sign and return all tests, and ensure that our child reads at least 180 minutes every week.
- We will always make ourselves available to our children, the school, and address any concerns they may have.
- If our child will be absent from school due to illness, we will notify the teacher prior to the start of school.
- We will carefully read all correspondence sent home from school.
- We will allow our child to go on Academy field trips.
- We understand that our child must follow the Academy rules so as to protect the safety, interests, and rights of all individuals at the school.
- We, not the school, are responsible for the behavior and actions of our child.

STUDENT'S COMMITMENT

- I will arrive at the Academy by 7:55 a.m. and stay until 4:00 p.m. every day. School begins on July 21, 2003, and ends on June 17, 2004.
- I will do whatever it takes to learn. I will always work, think, and behave in the best way I know.
- I will complete all my homework every night, I will call my teacher if I have a problem with homework or a problem about coming to school, and I will raise my hand and ask questions if I do not understand something in class.
- If I make a mistake, I will tell the truth and accept personal responsibility for my actions.
- I will always behave in a respectful manner that protects the safety, interests, and rights of every individual at the Academy.
- I am responsible for my own behavior.

Appendix

Choice and Commitment

One of our principal beliefs is that it is a choice to be part of the program. Over the past two school years, **97% of our fourth graders have chosen to return to the Academy for fifth grade.**

Academy Student Demographics

Ethnicity	Percent
African American	8
Asian Indian	3
Caucasian	35
Chinese	2
Filipino	17
Hispanic	11
Korean	6
Middle Eastern	8
Vietnamese	4
Other	6

English Language Learners	13
GATE	11
RSP	4

Respect and Responsibility

The Los Pen Academy expects their students to demonstrate high levels of respect and responsibility both inside and outside of class.

The students are responsible for homework completion every night. Their teachers are on call from 6 a.m. until 9 p.m. each day for questions on homework. Therefore, there are no excuses for not getting their homework done on a regular basis. **The Academy student homework completion rate is over 99%!**

The respectful attitudes of the Academy students have lead to responsible behavior. During the 2002-2003 school year, none of the 95 Academy students have received behavior referrals!

Student Success Team Meeting Notes

Los Peñasquitos Elementary School

Student:	Birthdate:	Parent(s):
Teacher:	Age:	Address:
Phone:	Grade:	Facilitator:
Persons Present:	Meeting Date:	Previous SST: ___Yes ___No

Background and Information	Strengths	Areas of Focus
Prior Strategies	**Action Plan**	**Responsible Person(s) / Timeline** **Tentative Follow-up Date:**

The Pyramid of Interventions

Adlai Stevenson High School

The strategies that appear in the pyramid on page 210 are listed in the recommended order, beginning at the bottom of the pyramid. Freshman Advisory and the Freshman Mentor Program are the first interventions, while special education placement is the final intervention.

The order of the strategies can be adjusted depending on the individual needs of the student. The number of students involved at each level should diminish as intervention strategies approach the apex of the pyramid.

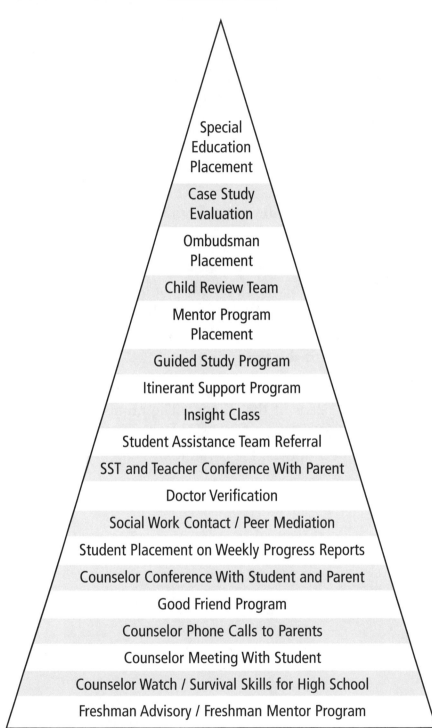

Special Education Placement

Case Study Evaluation

Ombudsman Placement

Child Review Team

Mentor Program Placement

Guided Study Program

Itinerant Support Program

Insight Class

Student Assistance Team Referral

SST and Teacher Conference With Parent

Doctor Verification

Social Work Contact / Peer Mediation

Student Placement on Weekly Progress Reports

Counselor Conference With Student and Parent

Good Friend Program

Counselor Phone Calls to Parents

Counselor Meeting With Student

Counselor Watch / Survival Skills for High School

Freshman Advisory / Freshman Mentor Program

Counselor Watch Program Letter

Adlai Stevenson High School

January 2004

Dear Middle School Principal:

Once again it is time to begin the Counselor Watch Program. I am looking forward to working with you to help your students make a smooth transition to Stevenson.

The focus of the Counselor Watch Program is to identify students who may have difficulty making the transition to high school for several different reasons. These may include poor academic progress, personal or family problems (including family member illness, divorce, non-custodial parent court orders, and so on), discipline infractions, or other problems listed on the enclosed referral sheets. Special education students who will continue to receive support at Stevenson should be included only if you feel that the counselor, dean, and/or social worker need to be aware of specific concerns.

We will continue the format of providing you with the forms to be completed prior to meeting with Stevenson staff. I've also enclosed an explanation of the various interventions used at Stevenson.

I will be contacting you in March to arrange the meeting, which we would like to hold in April. Please have Section One of the Counselor Watch Forms completed prior to our meeting and invite appropriate staff to join us. It would be helpful to have an extra copy of the completed forms so that we can make notes on them as we are discussing the students. It would also be helpful to have copies of grade reports because grades are used as one criterion for some of the programs.

In addition to identifying students for the Counselor Watch Program, we would also like to know which students would be appropriate for our summer school Survival Skills for High School class. The criteria include two Ds or worse on an ongoing basis. Although this class is not limited to regular education students, students who are struggling academically and/or socially and are <u>not</u> receiving special education services are our targeted population. If you are aware of any students at this time who may be appropriate for the class, please let me know now since space is limited. Please send the list to me by fax, e-mail, or mail before January 23 so that counselors will have the information when they register eighth graders for high school in February.

I would like to thank you in advance for your valuable assistance and input. As a result of your information over the years, we have been proactive in providing students with the appropriate interventions and support that have been crucial to their success in high school. Please feel free to contact me if you have any questions or concerns.

Sincerely,

_____

Counselor Watch Coordinator

Counselor Watch Referral Sheet

**This form is confidential. Do not copy or keep in student file.
This information is strictly off the record.**

Section I (to be completed prior to meeting with Stevenson)

Priority (3 = highest): 3   2   1

Reason for Referral:

___ Poor academic progress

___ Personal or family problems

___ Poor attendance and/or truancy

___ Low self-esteem

___ Peer relationship problems

___ Chronic underachiever

___ Discipline issues

___ Removed from special education

When?_____

Why?_____

___ Health issues (including medications)

___ Medications: _____

_____

___ Social work services

___ Alcohol/drug use

___ Possession/use in school

___ Possession/use in community

___ Strong suspicion/high risk

___ Suspicion of family use

___ Other:_____

Junior High School Programs/Interventions Provided:

_____

_____

_____

Current Services:
___LD ___BD ___Speech ___ESL ___504/Reason: _____ Other: _____

Section II (to be completed during meeting)

Stevenson Interventions:

___ Good Friend Program	___ Summer Survival Skills for High School
___ Weekly Eligibility Report	___ Counselor Check In
___ Guided Study	___ Dean
___ Mentor Program	___ Nurse
___ ISP	___ Social Work Services/Group
___ Other:_____	___ Student Assistance Coordinator

_____
Person Completing Report   Date

Good Friend Program Letter

Adlai Stevenson High School

CONFIDENTIAL

Date: September 2003

To: Teacher

From: Counselor

Thank you very much for your willingness to participate in the Good Friend Program. It is teachers like you who make this program so successful. Last year, 118 staff members became "Good Friends" to over 196 students in the school and more students are in need this year—in fact, over 200 students have been recommended for the program.

I have matched you with the following student for the Good Friend Program. This student has been identified by the Student Services Team as a student who is at risk based on information we received from the middle school through the Counselor Watch Program. Your assigned student is:

_____.

Remember, you need only pay a bit of extra attention to the student, take an interest in the student, and spend a few extra minutes once in a while with the student (before class, after class, before school, and so on).

The student <u>should not</u> know that he or she has been identified for special attention. There will be no write-ups, no assessments, or no specific number of minutes required to meet with each student.

The goal of the program is to encourage, support, and pay special attention to a student who may be experiencing low self-esteem, academic difficulty, or social/emotional concerns and is not currently in any other support program at Stevenson. We feel that the extra attention is just what the student needs. If you develop insights regarding the student that you feel may help us meet his or her needs, or if you feel he or she might need more support, please let me know.

I am available to you at any time. If you can't get to my office to see me, just drop me a note, e-mail, or call me, and I will get in touch with you during a non-class period.

Thank you again for your help. This program would not be possible without you.

Summer Skills Class Letter to Parents

Adlai Stevenson High School

May 2004

To the Parents of _____:

In order to give your son or daughter every opportunity to succeed at Stevenson High School, we would like to encourage you to enroll your student in a summer school program at Stevenson. The Survival Skills for High School Program is designed to assist students who may have had a history of achieving below their academic potential. These students may not show much interest in school and/or may need help with time management, note taking, test taking, study skills, reading comprehension, communication skills, and listening skills.

This class is included in the 2004 Summer School Program booklet and will be held for 4 weeks. It will be offered at two different times. The first session will meet from June 10 to July 3, and the second session will meet from July 8 to July 31. The class will meet from 8:10 a.m. to 12:30 p.m. Students who successfully complete this course will earn one high school credit. Please see the course description included in this letter for further information.

If you are interested in this course, please fill out the enclosed registration form, and return it as soon as possible to Stevenson High School, Attention Summer School Registration. You may also register by calling our Summer School office at 847-634-4000, ext. 1326, or by coming to Room 6036 at Stevenson to register in person. Should you need assistance with the tuition for the course, the Stevenson Community Foundation will assume responsibility for the cost. We feel that this course can make a difference in your student's transition to high school, and we hope you will enroll him or her at your earliest convenience.

Sincerely,

_____

Counselor

Course Description: Survival Skills for High School

<u>Time:</u> 8:10 a.m. to 12:30 p.m.

<u>MNT09S:</u> June 10 to July 3

<u>MNT10S:</u> July 8 to July 31

<u>Credit:</u> 1 per Semester, Pass/Fail

<u>Cost:</u> $170 per Semester

<u>Prerequisite:</u> This course is for incoming freshmen who experienced academic difficulties in junior high school or who may need assistance with the transition to high school.

<u>Class Enrollment:</u> Ninth-Grade Students

<u>Description:</u> This course provides an opportunity for students to review, refine, and build the skills necessary to succeed in high school. Instruction will occur in the areas of time management, listening skills, note taking, test taking, reading for comprehension, communication skills, goal setting, and building self-esteem. Included in this course will be an orientation to Adlai E. Stevenson High School, its programs, and its resources.

The Freshman Mentor Program

Adlai Stevenson High School

The Role of the Faculty Advisor and the Guidance Counselor

The upperclassmen mentors in the Stevenson program are aided by two faculty members: a faculty advisor and guidance counselor. The faculty advisor is in the Freshman Mentor Program (FMP) every day and assumes the role of the supervisor. The guidance counselor is in the FMP once a week and is the assigned guidance counselor for every freshman in that FMP.

The Faculty Advisor . . .

- Aids the student mentors in any way necessary

- Supplies the necessary supervision for a class of students

- Monitors the progress reports and report cards of each student and offers encouragement and advice

- Can organize, help with, and participate in activities

- Performs all administrative duties associated with a class (attendance and so on)

- Speaks with students when they have questions or concerns

- Is able to get to know more students outside of the traditional classroom interaction

The Guidance Counselor . . .

- Is able to meet and become acquainted with his or her incoming students

- Is able to talk about necessary topics (credits, electives, courses, and so on) with the students as a group

- Is provided time to answer questions for students who may not be able to schedule time at his or her office

- Gets to know the students better so they are more comfortable if they need to meet the counselor outside of advisory

FMP Faculty Advisor Expectations

1. Effective advisories are developed by strong faculty leadership. You must attend advisory Monday through Thursday and remind your director to arrange a substitute on days you are absent.

2. Daily attendance must be taken of your freshmen and mentors. If one of your student mentors is absent for any reason, be sure to mark him or her absent. If the absence is unauthorized, contact the attendance office.

3. Four Faculty FMP lunch meetings will be located in room 1123 on October 13, December 1, February 9, and May 11. Please be sure to attend. Your contribution at these meetings is invaluable.

4. It is important that you help to maintain a positive advisory atmosphere. It is your responsibility to ensure that your upperclassmen mentors are working effectively with their freshmen.

5. Please assist your counselor during his or her scheduled visits.

6. Please welcome visitors to your advisory. Typically you will be given advanced notification of visitors, but please be aware that they may visit your advisory without previous notification.

The advisory program is a critical component in our efforts to assist students with the transition to high school and to monitor their academic achievement and emotional well-being on a timely basis. As an advisor, you play a major role in our effort to promote success for every student. Please embrace the significance of that role and remember that this assignment is not designed to be teacher work time.

Goal Setting Worksheet

Adlai Stevenson High School

Student Name _____ ID _____ Date _____

	Short Term (this year)	Short Term (this year)	Long Term (1–4 years)
Personal Goals			
Academic Goals			
Co-Curricular/ Athletic Goals			
Student Responsibility Goals			

Original: Student   Canary: Counselor   Pink: Advisory Teacher

Co-Curricular Sign-Up Sheet

Adlai Stevenson High School

Please print your name and ID number clearly:

Name: _____

ID: _____

> The counselor will place a label with
> your name and ID number here.

Purpose

The purpose of this co-curricular sign-up sheet is to help you identify the clubs and activities that you might be interested in learning more about. The school district will give your name to the sponsor so that he or she can notify you when the first organizational meeting will take place at the beginning of the school year. Please keep in mind that you are **not** committing yourself to join these activities by completing this form.

Instructions

Please review the co-curricular handbook and then select up to three (3) activities from the co-curricular list. Copy the digit code number located next to the activity title from the co-curricular activities list in the handbook and print the number(s) in each box below. Here are a few examples for you to follow:

Examples

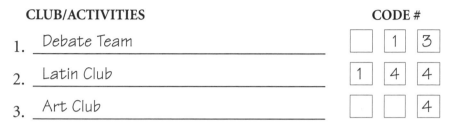

CLUB/ACTIVITIES		CODE #	
1. Debate Team			1 3
2. Latin Club		1 4 4
3. Art Club			4

Please Print Clearly and Fill in Your Choices Below

CLUB/ACTIVITIES   CODE #

1. _____   ☐ ☐ ☐

2. _____   ☐ ☐ ☐

3. _____   ☐ ☐ ☐

What Happens Next?

Your name will be given to the sponsor of the activity. The sponsor will communicate with you via United States mail during the summer with information about when the first organizational meeting will take place.

> **LEARN MORE ABOUT CLUBS AND ACTIVITIES, SPORTS TEAMS, AND INTRAMURALS BY COMING TO THE CO-CURRICULAR FAIR ON THURSDAY, MARCH 25, IN THE FIELD HOUSE.**

The Guided Study Program

Adlai Stevenson High School

Entrance Criteria

1. The student has received two or more grades of D on at least one report card.

2. A referral has been made by the Student Support Team.

3. The student is willing to abide by the terms of the Guided Study Contract.

4. The contract has been signed by the student, parent, and Guided Study teacher.

5. The student must meet with his or her counselor prior to placement in Guided Study.

Exit Criteria

A student may be removed from the Guided Study Program in one of two ways:

Option One (Student Must Meet Both Criteria)

- Student has passed all classes with a C or better.

- Student has expressed confidence in his or her ability to be successful without the program.

Option Two

- Student has failed to fulfill the Guided Study Contract. In this case, Guided Study is not an appropriate educational intervention and a referral to a more appropriate program will be made.

The Guided Study Teacher Will...

1. Have a concern for and interest in the success and well-being of each student.

2. Encourage students to organize their work and improve their study habits.

3. Encourage students to maintain grades of C or better.

4. Monitor student progress by reviewing mid-term reports and report cards when available.

5. Monitor usage of assignment notebooks.

6. Insist that students are engaged in constructive work each day.

7. Communicate with classroom teachers regarding student progress.

8. Provide academic support and assistance as needed.

9. Communicate with parents as needed.

10. Reinforce the importance of education.

(continued)

Student/Parent Contract for Admission Into the Guided Study Program

I. The Guided Study student will:

A. Bring school-related work and materials to Guided Study each day.

B. Maintain an assignment notebook.

C. Be actively engaged in the material brought to class and stay on task for the entire period.

D. Sustain appropriate behavior throughout the class period.

E. Agree to the above expectations and sign this form.

_____

Student Signature   Date

II. I have read the above and will encourage my child to maintain these expectations.

_____

Parent Signature   Date

III. If the contract is broken, the consequences will be:

A. Contact with the parent

B. A conference with the Guided Study teacher, student, and counselor

C. Removal from the Guided Study Program

Project PASS:
Preparing All Students for Success

Boones Mill Elementary School

PURPOSEFULLY ALIGN CURRICULUM, INSTRUCTION, ASSESSMENT, AND STAFF DEVELOPMENT

- Utilize State Resource Guides, The Virginia Standards of Learning (SOL) Blueprints, and Division Curriculum Guides to clarify essential knowledge and skills by grade level.

- Align daily instruction with specified learning objectives.

- Design and utilize teacher-made tests in the SOL Assessment format.

- Reinforce content and skills in "Specials" classes (i.e., Art, Music, Physical Education, Guidance, Library, Computers) and Pull-out Programs (i.e., Speech, Special Education Resource), and Cultural Arts Presentations.

- Provide staff with job-embedded opportunities for ongoing collaboration and professional development directly related to student achievement goals.

- Create a master schedule that provides protected instructional blocks, time for teacher collaboration, and individual teacher planning.

ACTIVELY PROMOTE A CLIMATE OF ACHIEVEMENT: INCENTIVES AND CELEBRATIONS

- Display a "Hand in Hand We All Learn" paper "people-chain" throughout the school, recognizing each student who meets specific academic goals.

- Recognize student curricular and non-curricular achievements on daily school announcements.

- Publish names of students who meet achievement goals in classroom and school newsletters.

- Provide individual student recognition in such areas as most improved, citizenship, and academic achievement in quarterly awards assemblies.

- Provide individual incentives and quarterly recognition assemblies for students who meet individual and classroom reading goals.

- Share professional learning and achievements at weekly team meetings and monthly staff meetings.

STRUCTURE STRONG PARENT PARTNERSHIPS

- Create systems for consistent, two-way communication between home and school (i.e., notes, phone calls, visits).

- Send student work folders home each week for parent review and signatures.

- Provide parents at each grade level with homework tips, study guides, and specific resource materials.

- Conduct grade-level parent workshops to clarify intended outcomes and provide strategies that enable parents to reinforce the intended learning at home.

SUPPORT STUDENTS WHO NEED ADDITIONAL TIME TO LEARN

- Conduct item analysis of student achievement data to identify individual and group strengths and weaknesses.

- Provide time and structure for students who need additional support to learn the intended skills/content.

- Create peer-tutoring systems within classrooms and grade levels.

- Implement a student buddy system to give younger students assistance from older students.

- Utilize staff to provide daily tutorial services for individual students and small groups.

- Utilize computer-based, individualized math and reading programs available in each classroom and computer lab.

- Organize parent volunteers, business partners, senior citizens, and high school and college interns to serve as mentors and tutors.

- Implement SOS Program—Save One Student—to provide personal encouragement and support to certain students.

- Convene the Child Study Team to plan additional interventions.

Parent/Student Guide to Fifth Grade Success

Boones Mill Elementary School

Created by Fifth Grade Teachers
Miss Tracy Anderson, Mrs. Beth Barksdale,
Mrs. Bernice Cobbs, and Mrs. Anne Harrison

*It's the dream of every parent
for each child to be given the chance
to fulfill his or her potential.*

*It's the goal of every teacher
to have a classroom of students who learn,
are challenged, and achieve.*

Upon entering the fifth grade, your child should be able to:

Math

❏ Recall multiplication facts from 1–12

❏ Solve problems involving addition and subtraction of money amounts and make change

❏ Tell time to the nearest minute, and identify equivalent periods of time (relationships among days, months, and years, as well as minutes and hours)

❏ Read a thermometer

❏ Solve word problems involving more than one process ($+, -, \times, \div$)

Reading

❏ Recognize fiction versus nonfiction

❏ Use dictionary skills (being able to look up the definition of a word)

❏ Know the main idea of a story versus the details of a story

❏ Summarize what has been read

❏ Identify synonyms (words that mean the same), antonyms (words that are opposite), homophones (words that sound the same, but have different meanings), and homographs (words that are written the same, but have different meanings)

Writing

❏ Write a complete sentence

❏ Identify and apply the parts of speech (noun, verb, adjective, and adverb)

❏ Write a multi-paragraph paper focused on a central idea

❏ Effectively use the writing process: brainstorming, drafting, proofreading, editing, and publishing

❏ Demonstrate the correct usage of grammar: subject-verb agreement, use of "I," double negative

Social Studies

❏ Identify the time periods of specific historical events: Columbus—1400s, Jamestown—1600s, Revolutionary War—1700s, Civil War—1800s

❏ Identify 20th Century Virginians: Arthur Ashe, Woodrow Wilson, Douglas Wilder, Harry F. Byrd

❏ Identify regions of Virginia: Tidewater, Piedmont, Ridge and Valley, Allegheny Plateau

Science

❏ Identify and apply the Scientific Method (question, hypothesis, experiment, analysis, and conclusion)

❏ Identify living processes (animals and plants)

❏ Identify and apply Earth systems (weather, solar system, earth, moon, and sun relation, electricity, and machines)

❏ Identify Virginia natural resources: plants, animals, watersheds, and rocks in Virginia

What should my child be able to do by the end of fifth grade?

Math

• Identify place value (read, write, identify, and compare)

• Add, subtract, multiply, and divide whole and decimal numbers

- Add and subtract with fractions and mixed numbers

- Describe and determine perimeter and area

- Identify and describe diameter, radius, chord, and circumference of a circle

- Choose an appropriate measuring device and unit of measure for length, weight, liquid volume, area, and temperature

- Determine elapsed time in hours and minutes

- Classify, measure, and draw angles and triangles (right, acute, obtuse)

- Identify and locate coordinate points (as in the game Battleship)

- Solve problems involving probability

- Collect and organize data using a variety of graphs

- Find the mean (average) and mode of a set of data

- Recognize and continue numeric and geometric patterns

- Use a variable to solve a problem

Reading/Literature

- Read and learn the meanings of unfamiliar words using knowledge of root words, prefixes, and suffixes as well as dictionary, glossary, and thesaurus

- Read a variety of literary forms

- Describe character development, plot, and conflict resolution

- Read and demonstrate comprehension of a variety of literary forms

Writing

- Write for a variety of purposes (describe, inform, entertain, and explain)
- Organize information
- Use vocabulary effectively
- Vary sentence structure
- Revise for clarity
- Edit for grammar, capitalization, spelling, and punctuation

Research

- Gather and use information from a variety of resources
- Skim materials to get a general overview or locate specific information
- Develop notes
- Organize and record information on charts, maps, and graphs
- Use electronic databases to access information
- Credit secondary sources

Science

- Use the Scientific Method to gather, organize, analyze, apply, and record data
- Understand how sound is transmitted
- Understand the basic characteristics of white light
- Understand that matter is anything that has mass, takes up space, and occurs as a solid, liquid, or gas
- Understand that organisms are made of cells and have distinguishing characteristics
- Understand characteristics of the ocean environment

- Understand how the Earth's surface is constantly changing (rock cycle, earthquakes, volcanoes, weathering, erosion, and human impact)

English

- Oral Language

- Participate in and contribute to discussions across content areas

- Organize information to present reports

- Maintain eye contact with listeners, use gestures to support message

- Make a planned oral presentation, summarize main points, use visual aids

Social Studies

- Describe life in America before the 17th Century

- Trace the routes and evaluate early explorations of the Americas

- Describe colonial America

- Analyze the United States Constitution and the Bill of Rights

- Describe challenges faced by the United States government

- Describe growth and change in America from 1801 to 1861

- Identify patriotic causes, key events, and effects of the Civil War and Reconstruction

- Interpret patriotic slogans and excerpts from notable speeches and documents in United States history up to 1877

- Develop skills in discussion, debate, and persuasive writing by analyzing historical situations and events

How Parents Can Help

✓ Continue to read aloud to your child.

✓ Encourage your child to read independently.

✓ Help your child develop critical reading skills through questioning.

✓ Require regular attendance in school.

✓ Encourage good study habits.

✓ Be familiar with the curriculum associated with your child's classes and grades.

✓ Talk to your child about what he or she is learning in specific subjects.

✓ Expect homework of some kind to be done every night.

✓ Set aside a specific time for homework.

✓ Ask questions about your child's homework.

✓ See that your child brings home and reviews class notes and other work done in school that day.

✓ Help your child balance study time with recreational time.

✓ Think of activities your child can do at home that relate to information being taught in school.

✓ Help your child apply his or her school learning to real-life situations in the news or life.

✓ Emphasize the importance of high academic achievement. Let your child know that you understand that tests may be challenging, but that taking them provides the opportunity to show how much he or she has learned.

✓ Be supportive and encouraging.

Essential Questioning

Asking your child questions about what has been read or studied is a key component to understanding with depth. A person who reads the words, thinks about their meaning, and then goes on to question will understand the most. Here are some specific questions that your child could answer orally or in writing.

Questions for Reading

Character Questions

- Who is the main character? Give a description.

- Does the main character seem to be a real person? How do you know?

- How are you like or different from the character in this story?

- What problem or conflict does the character face?

- What is the character's main goal?

- How many supporting characters does the author include in the story? Which characters support the main character?

- Who is/are the secondary character(s)? How do you know?

- Why did the main character act as he or she did when a certain event happened?

- Is the main character a flat character? A flat character is a character that does not change through the story. How do you know?

- Is the main character a developing character? Developing characters change at some point in the story. How do you know?

- Does the main character change over the course of the story? How?

Setting Questions (about the time and place in which story events occur)

- What is the setting for the story? Describe it in detail.

- Does the setting influence the mood the author is trying to create?

- Is the setting necessary for plot development?

- Does the author use many descriptive words to describe the setting? Name some of the words.

- Does weather play an important role in this story? Explain.

- Is the setting important to the story, or could this story take place anywhere?

Theme Questions (about major ideas about life or the message of a story)

- What is the most important idea, message, or lesson the author is trying to get across in the story?

- Is the theme clearly stated or is it implied?

- What does the story mean to you?

- Does this story have one theme or several? What is the theme(s)?

- What events and/or information from the story help you to make a conclusion about the theme?

Point of View Questions (a story is usually told from one standpoint)

First person point of view: A character in the story uses "I," "me," or refers to himself or herself.

Third person point of view: The narrator is outside the story, usually the author.

- Who is telling the story? How do you know?
- Who do the *I, me, my* refer to?
- From whose point of view are we experiencing the setting? How do you know?
- From whose point of view are we experiencing the plot? How do you know?

Plot Questions (the series of related events that happen in a story)

- What is the climax, the most exciting part, of the story?
- What is the conflict (problem) to be solved?
- What are several events that lead up to the climax?
- What is the basic struggle in the story?
- Is there a conflict between two characters in this story?
- Is there a conflict between a character and nature?

General Questions

- How are conflicts within the chapter solved?
- What is a good summary for this chapter/selection/passage?
- What do you know about the story/passage/selection so far?
- What words are important to the chapter/passage/selection to make the reading flow as it does?

- Which words or phrases would be considered sensory words?

- Where are the opinions within the story/passage/selection? (Opinions cannot be proven.)

- Where are the facts within the story/passage/selection? (Facts can be proven.)

- What examples of cause-and-effect are within the story?

Question Starters for Social Studies

- Which of the following best describes . . . ?

- What was the primary purpose of . . . ?

- Who first suggested that . . . ?

- What would be considered a disadvantage for . . . ?

- What would be considered an advantage for . . . ?

- Which of the following would be the best solution for . . . ?

- The purpose of the . . . is to . . . ?

- What is a principal reason for . . . ?

- What is the difference between . . . ?

- What contributions did . . . make during . . . ?

- What are the essential ideas regarding . . . ?

Question Starters for Science

- What are you investigating?

- How will you conduct your investigation?

- How will you collect your data?

- What are the basic characteristics of . . . ?

- What distinguishing characteristics does . . . have?

- What are the basic features of ... ?

- What is the problem?

- If you had to do it all over again, what would you do differently?

- What is the definition of ... ?

- What are the facts about ... ?

- Explain the differences and/or similarities about ... ?

- How does ... work?

- How can you restate important details in a few words?

- What are the most important details and why?

- Is there another way to put these ... into groups or categories?

- What will happen based on this information? (predict)

- What data were collected? (explain)

The Save One Student (SOS) Program

Boones Mill Elementary School

Thank you for agreeing to be a special adult friend and encourager for a Boones Mill Elementary Student. Please review the following information.

Your Student's Name: _____

Homeroom Teacher: _____

Suggestions for Getting Started:

1. Talk with your student's homeroom teacher to receive input about your student.

2. Check with the homeroom teacher to arrange a time to meet with your student.

3. Allow your student to help you or another student in your classroom/department.

4. Upper grade SOS students can read to lower grade students or help with special jobs.

5. Remember to give praise for efforts and give encouraging words.

Guidelines for Working With Your Student:

1. **VERY IMPORTANT: No money, food, or gift items of any kind are to be given or exchanged.**

2. You should make 2 or 3 contacts with your student each week. The contact can be anytime during the day that is convenient to your schedule.

3. Remember your involvement with this student is **<u>confidential</u>**. The student should not have knowledge of your assignment to them.

4. Check with the student in regards to his or her homework. Do not be afraid to ask to see their homework or offer to help them with it.

Team Feedback Sheet

_____

Name of Team: _____

Meeting Date: _____

Team Goal(s): _____

_____

_____

_____

Team Members Present: **Team Members Absent:**
                                       (List reason for each absence)
_____   _____

_____   _____

_____   _____

_____   _____

_____   _____

Topics/Meeting Outcomes:

Questions/Concerns:

Administrator: _____
Date: _____

Critical Questions for Team Consideration

Team Name: _____

Team Leader: _____

Date: _____

Consider the following statements in relationship to your team and indicate the level to which the statement is descriptive of your team:

This is not true of our team.	*This is true of some but not all of the team.*	*Uncertain.*	*Our team has addressed this issue.*	*We have consensus and act in accordance with our consensus.*

1	2	3	4	5	6	7	8	9	10

1. _____ *Each member of our team is clear on the intended outcomes of our course in general as well as on the specific outcomes of each unit.*

2. _____ *We have aligned the outcomes of our course to state standards and to the high-stakes tests our students will take.*

3. _____ *We have identified the prerequisite knowledge and skills needed to master the intended outcomes of the course or unit.*

4. _____ We have identified strategies and created instruments to assess whether students have the prerequisite knowledge and skills.

5. _____ We have agreed on how to best sequence the content of the course to help students achieve the intended outcomes.

6. _____ We have agreed on the criteria we will use in judging the quality of student work in key areas of our course such as writing, speaking, and projects.

7. _____ We have taught students the criteria we will use in judging the quality of their work and have provided them with examples.

8. _____ We have developed frequent formative assessments that help us identify strengths and weaknesses of individual students.

9. _____ We have developed summative assessments that help us assess the strengths and weaknesses of our program.

10. _____ We have established the proficiency level we want all students to achieve on our assessments.

11. _____ We have identified content and/or topics that can be eliminated so we can devote more time to essential curriculum.

12. _____ We have analyzed student achievement data and established measurable team goals that we are working together to achieve.

13. _____ We have identified team norms or protocols to guide us in working together.

14. _____ We adhere to our team norms and evaluate our effectiveness as a team at least twice each year.

15. _____ We are continually looking for new ways to help students achieve at higher levels.

The Professional Learning Community Continuum

Element of a PLC	Pre-Initiation Stage	Initiation Stage	Developing Stage	Sustaining Stage
Overall PLC Development	The school has not yet begun to address the principle of a PLC.	An effort has been made to address the principle, but the effort has not yet begun to impact a "critical mass."	A critical mass has endorsed the principle. Members are beginning to modify their thinking and practice as they attempt to implement the principle. Structural changes are being made to align with the principle.	The principle is deeply embedded in the school's culture. It represents a driving force in the daily work of the school. It is so internalized that it can survive changes in key personnel.
Mission: Is it evident that learning for all is our core purpose?	No effort has been made to engage faculty in identifying what they want students to learn or how they will respond if students do not learn. School personnel view the mission of the school as teaching rather than learning.	An attempt has been made, typically by the central office, to identify learning outcomes for all grade levels or courses, but this attempt has not impacted the practice of most teachers. Responding to students who are not learning is left to the discretion of individual teachers.	Teachers are clear regarding the learning outcomes their students are to achieve. They have developed strategies to assess student mastery of these outcomes, they monitor the results, and they attempt to respond to students who are not learning.	Learning outcomes are clearly articulated to all stakeholders in the school, and each student's attainment of the outcomes is carefully monitored. The school has developed systems to provide more time and support for students experiencing initial difficulty in achieving the outcomes. The practices, programs, and policies of the school are continually assessed on the basis of their impact on learning. Staff members work together to enhance their effectiveness in helping students achieve learning outcomes.

Element of a PLC	Pre-Initiation Stage	Initiation Stage	Developing Stage	Sustaining Stage
Shared Vision: Do we know what we are trying to create?	No effort has been made to engage faculty in describing preferred conditions for their school.	A vision statement has been developed for the school, but most staff are unaware of, or are unaffected by it.	Staff members have worked together to describe the school they are trying to create. They have endorsed this general description and feel a sense of ownership in it. School improvement planning and staff development initiatives are tied to the shared vision.	Staff members routinely articulate the major principles of the shared vision and use those principles to guide their day-to-day efforts and decisions. They honestly assess the current reality in their school and continually seek effective strategies for reducing the discrepancies between the conditions described in the vision statement and their current reality.
Shared Values: How must we behave to advance our vision?	Staff members have not yet articulated the attitudes, behaviors, or commitments they are prepared to demonstrate in order to advance the mission of learning for all and the vision of what the school might become. If they discuss school improvement, they focus on what other groups must do.	Staff members have articulated statements of beliefs or philosophy for their school; however, these value statements have not yet impacted their day-to-day work or the operation of the school.	Staff members have made a conscious effort to articulate and promote the attitudes, behaviors, and commitments that will advance their vision of the school. Examples of the core values at work are shared in stories and celebrations. People are confronted when they behave in ways that are inconsistent with the core values.	The values of the school are embedded in the school culture. These shared values are evident to new staff and to those outside of the school. They influence policies, procedures, and daily practices of the school as well as day-to-day decisions of individual staff members.

Element of a PLC	Pre-Initiation Stage	Initiation Stage	Developing Stage	Sustaining Stage
Goals: What are our priorities?	No effort has been made to engage the staff in setting and defining school improvement goals related to student learning. If goals exist, they have been developed by the administration.	Staff members have participated in a process to establish goals, but the goals are typically stated as projects to be accomplished or are written so broadly that they are impossible to measure. The goals do not yet influence instructional decisions in a meaningful way.	Staff members have worked together to establish long- and short-term improvement goals for their school. The goals are clearly communicated. Assessment tools and strategies have been developed and implemented to measure progress toward the goals.	All staff pursue measurable performance goals as part of their routine responsibilities. Goals are clearly linked to the school's shared vision. Goal attainment is celebrated and staff members demonstrate willingness to identify and pursue challenging stretch goals.
Collaborative Culture: Teachers Working Together	Teachers work in isolation. There is little awareness of what or how colleagues are teaching.	Teachers recognize a common curriculum that they are responsible for teaching, but there is little exchange of ideas regarding instructional materials, teaching strategies, or methods of assessment.	Teachers function in work groups that meet periodically to complete certain tasks such as reviewing intended outcomes and coordinating calendars.	Teachers function as a team. They work collaboratively to identify collective goals, develop strategies to achieve those goals, gather relevant data, and learn from one another. Unlike a work group, they are characterized by common goals and interdependent efforts to achieve those goals.
Collaborative Culture: Administrator/Teacher Relations	Questions of power are a continuing source of controversy and friction. Relationships between teachers and administrators are often adversarial.	Efforts have been made to reduce friction by clarifying management rights and teacher rights. Both parties are protective of intrusion onto their turf.	Administrators solicit and value teacher input as improvement initiatives are developed and considered, but administrators are regarded as having primary responsibility for school improvement.	Staff are fully involved in the decision-making processes of the school. Administrators pose questions, delegate authority, create collaborative decision-making processes, and provide staff with the information, training, and parameters they need to make good decisions. School improvement is viewed as a collective responsibility.

Element of a PLC	Pre-Initiation Stage	Initiation Stage	Developing Stage	Sustaining Stage
Parent Partnerships	There is little or no effort made to cultivate a partnership with parents. Parents are either ignored or viewed as adversaries.	An effort is made to keep parents informed of events and situations at school in order to secure parental support for the school's efforts.	Structures and processes for two-way communications with parents are developed. The parental perspective is solicited on both school-wide issues and matters related directly to their own children.	The school-parent partnership moves beyond open communication. The school provides parents with information and materials that enable parents to assist their children in learning. Parents are welcomed in the school and there is an active volunteer program. Parents are full partners in the educational decisions that affect their children. Community resources are used to strengthen the school and student learning.
Action Research	While individual teachers may try experiments in their own classrooms, no structures to support, assess, or share their findings are in place. Many staff members have no knowledge of or involvement in action research.	Some staff members participate in pilot action projects. The sharing of findings is largely informal.	Staff members have been trained in action research methods and conduct action research to improve their professional practice. Findings generated by this research are beginning to influence classroom practices.	Topics for action research arise from the shared vision and goals of the school. Staff members regard action research as an important component of their professional responsibilities. There are frequent discussions regarding the implications of findings as teachers attempt to learn from the research of their colleagues.

Element of a PLC	Pre-Initiation Stage	Initiation Stage	Developing Stage	Sustaining Stage
Continuous Improvement	Little attention is devoted to creating systems that enable either the school or individual teachers to track improvement. The school would have a difficult time answering the question, "Are we becoming more effective in achieving our shared vision?"	A few people in the school are tracking general indicators of achievement, such as mean scores on state and national tests. Positive trends are celebrated. Negative trends are dismissed or suppressed.	Individual teachers and teaching teams gather information that enables them to identify and monitor individual and team goals.	Everyone in the school participates in an ongoing cycle of systematic gathering and analysis of data to identify discrepancies between actual and desired results, goal setting to reduce the discrepancies, developing strategies to achieve the goals, and tracking improvement indicators.
Focus on Results	The results the school seeks for each student have not been identified.	Results have been identified, but are stated in such broad and esoteric terms that they are impossible to measure. Improvement initiatives focus on inputs—projects or tasks to be completed—rather than on student achievements.	Desired results have been identified in terms of student outcomes and student achievement indicators have been identified. Data are being collected and monitored within the school or district. Results of the analysis are shared with teachers.	Teams of teachers are hungry for information on results. Teachers themselves gather relevant data and use these data to identify improvement goals and to monitor progress toward goals.

References

Adams, J. (2004). Quote retrieved March 22, 2004, from http://www.brainyquote.com/quotes/quotes/j/johnquincy148359.html

Barth, R. (1991). Restructuring schools: Some questions for teachers and principals. *Phi Delta Kappan, 73*(2), 123–128.

Barth, R. (2001). *Learning by heart.* San Francisco: Jossey-Bass.

Bossidy, L., & Charan, R. (2002). *Execution: The discipline of getting things done.* New York: Crown Publishing.

Bottoms, G. (1998). *Things that matter most in improving student learning.* Atlanta: Southern Regional Education Board.

Bradley, A. (2000, October 4). Put to the test. *Education Week.* Retrieved April 13, 2004, from http://www.edweek.org/ew/ewstory.cfm?slug=05msfree.h20

Brookover, W., Beady, C., Flood, P., Schweitzer, J., & Wisenbaker, J. (1979). *School social systems and student achievement: Schools can make a difference.* New York: Praeger.

Burnette, R. (2002). How we formed our community. *Journal of Staff Development, 23*(1), 51–54.

Carnegie Foundation Council on Adolescent Development. (1989). *Turning points: Preparing American youth for the 21st Century.* New York: The Carnegie Corporation of New York.

Cole, R., & Schlechty, P. (1993). Teachers as trailblazers in restructuring. *Education Digest, 58*(6), 8–12.

Coleman, J. S., Cambell, E. Q., Hobson, C. J., McPartland. J., Mood, A. M., Weinfield, F. D., & York, R. L. (1966). *Equality of educational opportunity.* Washington, DC: U.S. Government Printing Office.

Collins, J. (2001). *Good to great! Why some companies make the leap . . . and others don't.* New York: Harper Business.

Collins, J., & Porras, J. (1994). *Built to last: Successful habits of visionary companies.* New York: Harper Collins.

Consortium on Productivity in the Schools. (1995). *Using what we have to get the schools we need.* New York: Teachers College Press.

Conzemius, A., & O'Neill, J. (2002). *The handbook for SMART school teams.* Bloomington, IN: Solution Tree (National Educational Service).

Covey, S. (2002). In Patterson, K., Grenny. J., McMillan, R., & Switzler, A. (2002). *Crucial conversations: Tools for talking when stakes are high.* New York: McGraw-Hill.

Cremin, L. (1964). *The transformation of the school: Progressivism in American education.* New York: Alfred Knopf.

Cubberly, E. (1909). *Changing conceptions of education.* Boston: Houghton-Mifflin.

Darling-Hammond, L. (1997). *The right to learn.* San Francisco: Jossey-Bass.

Darling-Hammond, L. (2004). Collaboration and development. *School Redesign Network.* Retrieved on March 21, 2004, from http://www.schoolredesign.net/srn/server.php?idx=228.

Drucker, P. (1996). *The leader of the future.* San Francisco: Jossey-Bass.

DuFour, R. (2000a). Living with paradox: A top ten list for principals. *Instructional Leader,* July, 3–5.

DuFour, R. (2000b). School leaders as staff developers. *Catalyst for Change, 29*(3), 13–15.

DuFour, R. (2000c). The superintendent as staff developer. *The School Administrator, 57*(8), 20–24.

DuFour, R. (2001). In the right context. *Journal of Staff Development, 22*(1), 14–17.

DuFour, R. (2002). The learning-centered principal. *Educational Leadership, 59*(8), 12–15.

DuFour, R. (2004a). Leadership is an affair of the heart. *Journal of Staff Development, 25*(1), 67–68.

DuFour, R. (2004b). The steps successful principals take to promote learning—for students and adults. *Instructional leader, 27*(2), 1–12.

DuFour, R. (2004c). The three big ideas that drive Professional Learning Communities. *Educational Leadership, 61*(8), in press.

DuFour, R., & Burnette, R. (2002). Pull out negativity by its roots. *Journal of Staff Development, 23*(3), 27–30.

DuFour, R., & DuFour, R. (2003). Building a professional learning community: Central office support for learning communities. *The School Administrator, 60*(5), 13–18.

DuFour, R., & Eaker, R. (1998). *Professional learning communities at work: Best practices for enhancing student achievement.* Bloomington, IN: Solution Tree (National Educational Service).

Eaker, R., DuFour, R., & DuFour, R. (2002). *Getting started: Reculturing schools to become professional learning communities.* Bloomington, IN: Solution Tree (National Educational Service).

Edmonds, R. (1982). Revolutionary and evolutionary: The Effective Schools movement. Retrieved March 19, 2004, from http://www.effectiveschools.com/freestuff.asp

Fullan, M. (1997). Emotion and hope: Constructive concepts for complex times. In A. Hargreaves (Ed.), *Rethinking educational change with heart and mind.* Alexandria, VA: Association for Supervision on Curriculum Development (ASCD).

Fullan, M. (1999). *Change forces: The sequel.* London: Falmer Press.

Fullan, M. (2001). *Leading in a culture of change.* San Francisco: Jossey-Bass.

Gardner, J. (1990). *On leadership.* New York: Free Press.

Gardner, J. (2004). Quote retrieved on March 22, 2004, from http://www.brainyquote.com/quotes/authors/j/john_w_gardner.html

Gonzalez, B. (2003, September 20). Striving for excellence: Academy pushes students to reach potential and beyond. *The San Diego Union-Tribune.*

Hamel, G. (2000). *Leading the revolution.* Boston: Harvard Business School Press.

Hargreaves, A. (2004). Broader purposes call for higher understanding: An interview with Dennis Sparks. *Journal of Staff Development, 25*(2), 46–50.

Herszenhorn, D. (2004, March 3). City plans to eliminate most middle schools. *The New York Times.* Retrieved March 10, 2004, from http://www.nytimes.com/2004/03/03/education/03SCHO.html

Hord, S. (1997). *Professional learning communities: Communities of continuous inquiry and improvement.* Austin, TX: Southwest Educational Development Laboratory. Retrieved on March 20, 2004, from http://www.sedl.org/pubs/change34/

IBM. (2003). Linux television commercial. Retrieved April 30, 2004, from http://www-3.ibm.com/e-business/doc/content/lp/prodigy.html

Jackson, A., & Davis, G. (2000). *Turning points 2000: Educating adolescents in the 21st Century.* New York: Teachers College Press.

James, J. (1995). *Thinking in the future tense.* Keynote address presented at the 1995 Annual Conference of the National Staff Development Council, Vancouver, Canada.

Jefferson, T. (1782). Bill on Education. Thomas Jefferson Digital Archive Number 2398. Charlottesville, VA: University of Virginia Library. Retrieved March 19, 2004, from http://etext.lib.virginia.edu/etcbin/foleydate-browse?id=1782.

Jefferson, T. (1816). Letter to Charles Yancey. Thomas Jefferson Digital Archive Number 2391. Charlottesville, VA: University of Virginia

Library. Retrieved March 19, 2004, from http://etext.lib.virginia.edu/etcbin/foleydate-browse?id=1816

Jenks, C., Smith, M. S., Ackland, H., Bane, M. J., Cohen, D., Grintlis, H., Heynes, B., & Michelson, S. (1972). *Inequality: A reassessment of the effects of family and schooling in America.* New York: Basic Books.

Journal of education. (1898). 47, 88.

Katzenbach, J., & Smith, D. (1993). *The wisdom of teams: Creating the high-performance organization.* New York: Harper Collins.

Kierkegaard, S. Quote retrieved March 22, 2004, from http://www.worldofquotes.com/author/Kierkegaard/1/

Kotter, J. (1996) *Leading change.* Boston: Harvard Business School Press.

Kouzes, J., & Posner, B. (1987). *The leadership challenge: How to get extraordinary things done in organizations.* San Francisco: Jossey-Bass.

Leavitt, F. (1912). *Examples of an industrial education.* Boston: Ginn and Company.

Lezotte, L. (1991a). *Correlates of effective schools: The first and second generation.* Effective Schools products. Retrieved on March 22, 2004, from http://www.effectiveschools.com/freestuff.asp

Lezotte, L. (1991b). *Learning for all.* Okemos, MI: Effective Schools products.

Lezotte, L. (2004). *Revolutionary and evolutionary: The Effective Schools movement.* Effective Schools products. Retrieved March 19, 2004, from http://www.effectiveschools.com/freestuff.asp

Lickona, T. (2004). *Character matters: How to help our children develop good judgment, integrity, and other essential values.* New York: Touchstone Books.

Louis, K. S., Kruse, S. D., & Marks, H. (1996). *Schoolwide professional community.* In F. M. Newmann (Ed.), *Authentic achievement: Restructuring schools for intellectual quality.* San Francisco: Jossey-Bass.

Marzano, R. (2003). *What works in schools: Translating research into action.* Alexandria, VA: Association for Supervision and Curriculum Development.

Maslow, A. (2004). Quote retrieved March 20, 2004, from http://www.quotationspage.com/quotes/Abraham_Maslow/

McLaughlin, M., & Talbert, J. (2001). *Professional learning communities and the work of high school teaching.* Chicago: University of Chicago Press.

National Association of Elementary School Principals. (2002). *Leading learning communities: Standards for what principals should know and be able to do.* Alexandria, VA: Author.

National Association of Secondary School Principals. (2002). *What the research shows: Breaking ranks in action.* Reston, VA: Author.

National Association of Secondary School Principals. (2004). *Breaking ranks II: Strategies for leading high school reform.* Reston, VA: Author.

National Center for Education Statistics. (2000). Years of school completed by persons aged 25 and over: 1910-1999. Retrieved March 19, 2004, from http://nces.ed.gov/programs/digest/d00/dt008.asp

National Commission on Education. (1983). *A nation at risk.* Washington, DC: U.S. Government Printing Office.

National Commission on Teaching and America's Future. (2003). *No dream denied: A pledge to America's children:* Washington, DC: Author.

National Education Association (1910). Report of the Commission on the Place of Industries in Public Education. (1974). In M. Lazerson & W. N. Grubs (Eds.), *American education and vocationalism: A documentary history.* New York: Teachers College Press.

National Forum to Accelerate Middle-Grades Reform. (2004). Retrieved March 19, 2004, from http:// www.mgforum.org/about/about.asp

National Middle School Association. (1982). *This we believe.* Columbus, OH: Author.

National Middle School Association. (1995). *This we believe: Developmentally responsive middle level schools.* Columbus, OH: Author.

National Middle School Association. (2003). *This we believe: Successful schools for young adolescents. An executive summary of a position paper.* Columbus, OH: Author. Retrieved March 20, 2004, from http://www.nmsa.org.

National Middle School Association. (2004). The NMSA positions statement on student achievement. Retrieved March 19, 2004, from http://www.nmsa.org.

National Staff Development Council. (2001). *Standards for staff development.* Oxford, OH: Author. Retrieved March 21, 2004, from http://www.nsdc.org/standards/learningcommunities.cfm.

Patterson, K., Grenny, J., McMillan, R., & Switzler, A. (2002). *Crucial conversations: Tools for talking when stakes are high.* New York: McGraw-Hill.

Peters, J., & Waterman, R. (1982). *In search of excellence: Lessons from America's best run companies.* New York: Harper and Row.

Reeves, D. (2002). *The leader's guide to standards: A blueprint for educational equity and excellence.* San Francisco: Jossey-Bass.

Reeves, D. (2004). *Accountability for learning: How teachers and school leaders can take charge.* Alexandria, VA: ASCD.

Richardson, J. (2004). *Learning from the inside out: Learning from positive deviance in your organization.* Oxford, OH: National Staff Development Council.

Rickover, H. G. (1959). *Education and freedom.* New York: E.P. Dutton.

Rose, L., & Gallup, A. (2002). The thirty-fourth annual PDK/Gallup poll of the public's attitude toward public school. *Phi Delta Kappa, 84*(1), 41–56.

Rutter, M. (1979). *Fifteen thousand hours: Secondary schools and their effects on children.* Cambridge, MA: Harvard University Press.

Schlecty, P. (1997). *Inventing better schools: An action plan for education reform.* San Francisco: Jossey-Bass.

Schmoker, M. (2001). *The results fieldbook: Practical strategies from dramatically improved schools.* Alexandria, VA: ASCD.

Schmoker, M. (2003). First things first: Demystifying data analysis. *Educational Leadership, 60*(5), 22–24.

Schmoker, M. (2004). Tipping point: From feckless reform to substantive instructional improvement. *Phi Delta Kappan, 85*(6), 424–432.

Schools to Watch. (2004a). Retrieved March 19, 2004, from http://www.schoolstowatch.org/what.htm

Schools to Watch. (2004b). Introduction to Freeport Intermediate School. Retrieved March 19, 2004, at http://www.schoolstowatch.org/freeport/fabout.htm

Schools to Watch. (2004c). Welcome to Freeport Intermediate School. Retrieved April 13, 2004, from http://www.schoolstowatch.org/freeport/

Senge, P. (1995). On schools as learning organizations: A conversation with Peter Senge by J. O'Neil. *Educational Leadership, 52*(7), 20–23.

Senge, P., Ross, R., Smith, B., Roberts, C., & Kleiner, A. (1994). *The fifth discipline fieldbook: Strategies and tools for building a learning organization.* New York: Doubleday.

Shaw, G. B. (1913). *Pygmalion.* London: Penguin.

Sparks, D. (2003, Winter). Change agent: An interview with Michael Fullan. *Journal of Staff Development, 24*(1), 55–58.

Stiggins, R. (2001). *Student involved classroom assessment, 3rd edition.* Upper Saddle River, NJ: Merrill Prentice-Hall.

Stiggins, R. (2002). Assessment crisis: The absence of assessment for learning. *Phi Delta Kappan, 83*(10), 758–767.

Stiggins, R. (2003, July). *New beliefs, better assessments.* Presented at the Professional Learning Communities at Work Institute, San Diego, CA.

Tichy, N. (1997). *The leadership engine: How winning companies build leaders at every level.* New York: Harper Business.

Valentine, J. (2004). "Highly effective middle schools and how they got that way." Presentation at the National Association of Secondary School Principals Annual Conference. Retrieved March 10, 2004, from http://www.mllc.org/presenta.htm

Video Journal of Education. (2001). *Leadership in the age of standards and high stakes: Building professional learning communities: Featuring Richard DuFour.* Sandy, UT: TeachStream.

Video Journal of Education. (2003). *Elementary principals as leaders of learners: Featuring Rebecca Burnette DuFour.* Sandy, UT: TeachStream.

Welter, R. (1963). *Popular education and democratic thought.* New York: Columbia University Press.

Yecke, S. (2003). *The war against excellence: The rising tide of mediocrity in America's middle schools.* Westport, CT: Greenwood Publishing.

Make the Most of Your Professional Development Investment

Let Solution Tree schedule time for you and your staff with leading practitioners in the areas of:

- **Professional Learning Communities** with Richard DuFour, Robert Eaker, Rebecca DuFour, and associates
- **Effective Schools** with associates of Larry Lezotte
- **Assessment *for* Learning** with Rick Stiggins and associates
- **Crisis Management and Response** with Cheri Lovre
- **Classroom Management** with Lee Canter and associates
- **Discipline With Dignity** with Richard Curwin and Allen Mendler
- **PASSport to Success** (parental involvement) with Vickie Burt
- **Peacemakers** (violence prevention) with Jeremy Shapiro

Additional presentations are available in the following areas:

- Youth at Risk Issues
- Bullying Prevention/Teasing and Harassment
- Team Building and Collaborative Teams
- Data Collection and Analysis
- Embracing Diversity
- Literacy Development
- Motivating Techniques for Staff and Students

Solution Tree
304 West Kirkwood Avenue
Bloomington, IN 47404
(812) 336-7700
(800) 733-6786 (toll free)
FAX (812) 336-7790
email: info@solution-tree.com
www.solution-tree.com

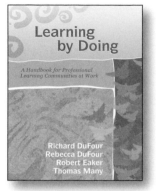

Learning by Doing
Richard DuFour, Rebecca DuFour,
Robert Eaker, and Thomas Many
Perplexing problems become workable solutions as collaborative teams take action to close the knowing-doing gap and transform their schools into PLCs. **BKF214**

Revisiting Professional Learning Communities at Work™: New Insights for Improving Schools
Richard DuFour, Rebecca DuFour, and
Robert Eaker
This 10th-anniversary sequel to *Professional Learning Communities at Work*™ offers advanced insights on deep implementation, the commitment/consensus issue, and the human side of PLC. **BKF252**

The Power of Professional Learning Communities at Work™: Bringing the Big Ideas to Life
Featuring Richard DuFour, Robert Eaker, and
Rebecca DuFour
This video series explores eight diverse schools, where teachers and administrators engage in candid conversations and collaborative meetings. See how successful schools radically improve student learning as you learn the fundamentals of PLC. **VIF094**

Professional Learning Communities at Work Plan Book
Rebecca DuFour, Richard DuFour, and Robert Eaker
With space for eight class periods, this process book helps teacher teams address crucial, PLC concepts. **BKF217**

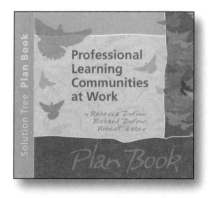